THROUGH EDITORS' EYES

The 1859 Revival in Ireland – as reported by the local press

To: Joe & Deborah

FROM: Austin & Elsie

With love.

Christmas, 2009.

THROUGH EDITORS' EYES

The 1859 Revival in Ireland – as reported by the local press

Selected and edited by Samuel Adams

Revival
PUBLISHING

THROUGH EDITORS' EYES

The 1859 Revival in Ireland – as reported by the local press

© 2009 Samuel Adams

Revival Publishing,
10 Kinallen Road,
Dromara,
Dromore,
BT25 2NL
Northern Ireland

www.revivalmovement.org

Acknowledgements

I would like to acknowledge the tremendous support and encouragement that I have received from my wife, Carol. Her patience throughout the months of research, editing, etc has been very much appreciated. I would also like to thank my family for all of their advice and guidance.

I am very grateful to Isobel Metcalfe who has worked extremely hard in the typing of the entire book and if it was not for her dedication this book would not have been produced.

John Law has spent many hours proof reading, checking and rechecking the entire script and I am more than grateful to him for his attention to detail. As he noted the corrections he would make the odd little note – 'This is fantastic' or 'I love this story' – his enthusiasm has been a source of inspiration to me.

I am also very grateful for the help of David and Heather Watson and Clive Allen in the reading, checking and their helpful advice in the production of this book. I would also like to thank the Directors and the staff of Revival Movement Association for their encouragement in this publication.

Victor Maxwell has written two books in connection with this ministry and we are grateful to him for writing the article on the reverse side of the cover.

We all know the importance of a good cover and I would like to thank our graphic designer Aramis Claudio de Barros who works so faithfully in the background.

Introduction

The revival during 1859 was a remarkable time of spiritual blessing among the people of Ireland, when many thousands came to know the Lord Jesus Christ as their personal Saviour. The impact was so noticeable that the newspapers began to write in detail, bringing up-to-date news concerning services and how the Lord was working. During the year, many column inches were taken up with news from all across the country. Newspaper editors frequently commented that they could bring only a selection of the news that they received concerning the revival, and in this book I have selected only a small portion of the material published during 1859.

Having read much of the day-by-day news, I noticed that certain observations came to the fore time after time. I want to highlight these and, as you read through these newspaper reports, I pray that you will also be blessed and challenged.

In many of the towns and villages where the Spirit of God moved we can see there was already a faithful minister preaching the Word of God. These were men who knew the Lord and men who were ready to reach out to others with the gospel message. When they preached they used straight talking language – Heaven and Hell were real places; when they preached people understood exactly where they stood in the light of eternity.

One of the great features during this time of spiritual revival was how the Spirit of God came and convicted people of their sinful state before a holy God. The awfulness of sin was very real and people were often burdened when they realised how they had sinned before the Lord. Cries for mercy were often heard, followed by the peace and joy that only Jesus Christ can give. Surely the Holy Spirit must have opened the eyes of people's understanding, to see spiritual truths that most of us can see only through a glass darkly.

Some people were convicted in what appeared to be a very sudden and dramatic way, yet many others were convicted and converted in a quiet, private manner. As you read through these accounts of the working of God, it can be easy to think that all cases of conviction were dramatic, but frequently the editors in one or two lines refer to many others who were convicted and converted quietly in services or at home.

New prayer meetings commenced with amazing speed – people were hungry for spiritual worship. As you look through your mind's eye you can imagine narrow streets in the city, where families lived in small houses, and yet doors were opened and friends invited in for prayer and fellowship. So many attended these meetings that in some places five or six prayer meetings could be held in the same street at the same time. No doubt as the people prayed, the Spirit of God continued to move through Ireland in an unparalleled way.

Throughout these newspaper reports we see that godly ministers of the gospel from different denominations set aside their differences and worked together as one during the revival. They preached, prayed and counselled together in many kinds of services, whether in the churches, homes or in the open air. It is also interesting to read how the ordinary men on the street fully approved of their ministers uniting in the work of the gospel.

Every work of God has its critics and this time of revival was no different. However, the evidence of changed lives was remarkable and convincing. People's lives were transformed so much so that the social life of communities was changed. For uncouth language and cursing to be seldom heard, to see Sunday as a day of worship, to see the public house emptied and closed, for the drunk to disappear from the street, leaves one filled with awe and wonder. Surely as we read these accounts of the work of God, our hearts will be stirred up to pray and long for a similar move of the Spirit of God in our own lives and in the lives of all around us.

Samuel Adams - 2009

"The Ballymena Observer" Saturday, 26th March 1859

"A public meeting, under the direction and management of the Presbyterian ministers, was convened by public notice and held in the 1st Presbyterian Church of Ahoghill, on the evening of March 14th on the subject of 'revivals'. The congregation attending was immense – hundreds were unable to obtain admittance and the new converts, from all parts of the neighbourhood, were present on the occasion.

"Soon after the commencement of the service an impulse to address the audience fell suddenly, and apparently with all the power of Prophetic inspiration, upon one of the 'converted' brethren. Every attempt to silence or restrain him was found utterly impossible. He declared that a revelation had been committed to him and that he spoke by the command of a Power superior to any ministerial authority. Defying every effort at control, he proceeded to expound religious phrases with a rapidity and fluency which caused intense astonishment and created a panic of very serious alarm among the audience. A rush was made towards the front of the galleries and, under an apprehension that they might collapse, the clergyman gave an order that the church should be immediately vacated.

"A scene of terrible confusion immediately ensued and, when the premises were ultimately cleared, the streets of Ahoghill presented another scene which defies all powers of description, and such as the oldest inhabitant had never seen. The leading convert, who is a comfortable farmer and a member of the congregation, assisted by several other speakers of the converted class, addressed the audience, numbering about three thousand and comprising people of every creed from Episcopalian to Roman Catholic. The chief speaker fervently proclaimed pardon to all sinners, inviting them to come forward and receive the Spirit of adoption, Whom he declared himself commissioned to impart, occasionally holding up his hands bidding the people to receive the Holy Ghost.

"The immense assembly appeared to be thoroughly paralysed. Amid a chilling rain, and on the streets covered with mud, fresh converts, moved by the passionate Apostolic language of the speaker, fell upon their knees in the attitude of prayer; a spark of electricity appeared to have stimulated and impressed a large number of the audience, and it is confidently confirmed that some, who went there to mock, were heard praying. These are the local effects of this extraordinary movement and the result is that the converts continued firmly rooted and grounded in the belief that they are under the immediate inspiration and guidance of the Divine Spirit. Their meetings multiplied in number and the 'new births', under the circumstances which I have already stated, are daily being increased."

"The Banner of Ulster" Saturday, 21st May 1859

The Religious Revivals near Ballymena

"The Rev. Frederick Buick read the following carefully prepared report, of the Presbytery of Ahoghill, on the state of religion before the senate of Ballymena and Coleraine, on Wednesday last:-

"'It is the privilege of the Presbytery to have to record, on this more than on former occasions, glad tidings of great joy. The Lord has been pleased to visit a large portion of our area with the welcoming showers of a gracious revival. Our churches have experienced an awakening, the most cheering in its character and holy in its fruits. Shortly after the beginning of the present year, the Lord was pleased to convert a family near Ahoghill and to bless their conversion in a large degree for promoting the conversion of others. An extraordinary interest began to be awakened; prayer meetings multiplied – crowds flocked to these refreshing streams – ordinary houses were unable to accommodate the eager multitudes who assembled to hear the burning prayers, and to listen to the plain but heart-stirring addresses of the converted brethren, and those ministers and laymen whose hearts the Lord moved to engage in this important work.

"'The open field and the public roadside, even in the cold evenings of spring, were the scenes of deeply interesting meetings, over which angels hovered with joy. The prayer meetings held in the First and Second Presbyterian Churches were crowded to excess, although held on the same evening and at the same hour. For several miles around, multitudes flocked to these meetings for prayer and exhortation. Our lay brethren from Connor, at the first gave, and continue from time to time to give, a powerful momentum to the good work.

"'Never in these localities was there such a time of secret and public prayer. In all directions prayer meetings have sprung up and that without number. They are conducted in a manner of deepest solemnity, and with a burning earnestness for the outpouring of the Holy Ghost and for the conversion of souls. These meetings have been significantly honoured by the Lord. The Spirit had descended in power. Through the instruction of the Word and prayer, convictions – often the most powerful, even to the convulsing of the whole frame, the trembling of every joint, intense burning of heart and complete loss of strength – have been produced.

"'The arrow of conviction pierces the conscience, the heart swells near to bursting, a heavy and intolerable burden presses down the spirit, and the burdened, burning heart, unable to contain any longer, bursts forth in the piercing cry of distress, saying, 'Lord Jesus, have mercy on my sinful soul.' This is the similar experience of the old and of the young – of the strong man and the delicate woman. Under such convictions, the heart finds relief in pouring out its cries and tears before the Lord. These convictions are followed by hours of kneeling before the Lord, crying, confessing sin, begging for mercy and beseeching the Lord to come to the heart. This is done in tones of deepest sincerity and in utterances of the most passionate earnestness. It may be days, or weeks, or even months, with convictions returning, more or less powerfully, in the constant duty of prayer, and in the reading of the Word, before a calm and gentle peace in believing is enjoyed.

"'There does not appear to be any fanaticism manifested, any heresy broached, any self-righteousness exhibited, or any sectarianism shown. A few interesting cases, of the conviction and conversion of Roman Catholics, have occurred. It is worthy of note that under the light and power of this movement, they love the Bible, pore over its sacred pages, pray through the prevailing Name of Jesus alone, place reliance on Christ alone for their salvation and, in the exercise of their religious liberty, join the worship of a purer Church.

"'The whole intellectual and moral being is powerfully stirred. Under the awakening of an inactive mind, the stirring up of the slumbering conscience, the powerful movement of the nervous system, the imagination is often active picturing out solemn scenes of the future and in hearing words of warning and counsel. Such sights and sounds are easily accounted for, while they are often blessed, producing saving impressions. Two great truths take full possession of the mind, namely – man is a sinner, under judgement, unto condemnation; and, Jesus is the Almighty Saviour to deliver, and faith in Him the way of obtaining that deliverance.

"'Convictions have taken place on a large scale, and conversions have followed. Many – even hundreds – are giving the most satisfying evidence of being in Christ – of drunkards, blasphemers, card players, Sabbath-breakers, neglecters of ordinances, and the wicked in general. It may be truly said, 'They are now, in Christ, new creatures.' With them old things are passed away and all things have become new. This is not an appearance put on but, as far as yet known, a deep and abiding reality. Sin – besetting sin – is crucified. One man, well-known for cursing and blasphemy, now declares that he never feels the slightest temptation to return to his former sin. Another, notorious for his love of strong drink, now says that he shudders at the sight of a public house. The love for playing cards is now transferred to his Bible. Obscene songs have given place to songs of Zion. Scenes of contention are exchanged for scenes of prayer, and praise, and the reading of the Word.

"'Wild, wicked, and godless characters, whom no human power could remodel, are now to be seen sitting at the feet of Jesus, clothed, and in their right mind. They are walking with Christ, caring for the one thing needful and living for the noblest object of life – the glory of God. This is the case not in solitary incidents, but in hundreds – not merely with the young, just initiated into a course of sin, but with the old, confirmed in their sinful habits. Public and prevailing sins have been powerfully curbed.

"'In those favourite districts, where this blessed work has taken deepest root and is transferring influences being most widely felt, drunkenness, Sabbath-breaking, blasphemy, profane language and neglect of the great salvation, have all been eradicated. The tone of public morals is enlightened, sanctified and elevated. The things of God are the subjects of daily, normal conversation.

"'Groups may be seen around our churches, during the same hour, at the corners of our streets, with their Bibles in their hands, seeking for the meaning of some portion of the Divine Word. The singing of Psalms may be heard in all directions. In many localities, profane songs are idle amusements which cannot be endured. While attending the largest prayer meetings of assembled thousands, and retiring from them at whatever hour, there is no levity, no improprieties, but an all-prevailing seriousness to be witnessed. On this revival work, so far as it has as yet developed itself, there is written, 'Holiness to the Lord.'

"'Even upon the portion of the public who make no claim to be religious, a deep solemn influence has been exercised. Many of them are thoughtful and enquiring, attending the prayer meetings with evident interest and, it is to be hoped, with benefit. But among the awakened, and converted, already delightful fruits are growing up with rapidity to maturity.

"'Prayer has received a powerful stimulus. Not only secret, but family and public prayer is one of those heavenly fruits. It is truly astonishing the liberty that many – very many – both male and female, have got in public prayer. It is most refreshing to hear the holy, earnest, edifying prayers which many babes in Christ are now offering at the family altar and at the public prayer meetings. It is not uncommon to hear the voice of prayer waft from an adjoining field.

"'In the class of young communicants, preparing to go up for the first time to the table of the Lord, it is delightful to hear one after another praying, in words that burn, at the mercy seat.

"'At the conclusion of a public prayer meeting, on a Saturday evening in his district, a blind boy, taught in the Belfast Institution for the deaf and dumb and the blind, whose heart was stirred, could not let the meeting separate without calling attention to the following day – the solemn privilege of the Lord's Supper among them; and they offered up the most earnest prayer of faith, that the Holy Spirit might descend upon them and that the communion might be a season of gracious revival.

"'The Bible is studied, prized, and loved, more than it ever was before. It is felt to be 'more precious than gold, yea, than much fine gold and to be sweeter than honey, yea, than the honey that droppeth from the comb.' Several, who were staying away from services where the gospel was preached, had been moved to the House of God, in whatever attire they could command, though they were poor; where others had been stirred to obtain decent clothes, who are now to be seen reverently worshipping in the House of God, but they had not been there for years before.

"'Many, too, have been to keep the feast of the Lord's Supper, in obedience to the dying command of the Lord. Our congregation never had such an appearance before, of enthusiastic, earnest worshippers. Love to Jesus is another of the precious fruits of this revival. This is expressed in tones, in words that cannot be mistaken; nor is there any reason to doubt its reality. The Lord is filling the thoughts of the enthroned, and in the affections of the converted, as 'The Chiefest among ten thousand and altogether lovely.' Love to the brethren is a very prominent feature of the new and divine life that is awakened. They love one another fervently. Their desire is to visit friends and relatives, talk with them about the concerns of their souls, and exhort them to flee from the wrath to come. With great sincerity they plead them to seek Jesus, and that now, without a moment's delay, while He is waiting to be gracious. Of this may be said, 'being made free from sin, and become servants to God, ye have your fruit unto holiness, and the end everlasting life', nor are the fruits of this revival confined to the convicted and converted. There are thousands of the surrounding Christian population who are revived and refreshed as parched corn, in the long drought of summer, after the sending of the cooling and invigorating shower. There is a quickening to duty, to spirituality, to communion with God, which is manifest and delightful. Never in this locality were there such holy, persistent, and believing prayers offered up by members, in the Name of the holy child Jesus, for the outpouring of the Holy Ghost.

"'This gracious revival has extended from the parish of Connor to that of Ahoghill, then to Portglenone, and round by Tully, Largey, Grange, Straid, Slatt, Galgorm Park, Killalers, Cloughwater, Clough, and Rasharkin. Nor is it yet showing any symptoms of decline – on the contrary, it is moving on with amazing Power. Every day, and almost every hour is bringing tidings of conviction. The interest is more and more awakening and extending.

"'The means by which this blessed work is carried are in no way extraordinary. Prayer and praise, the reading of the Word, and plain, pointed, solemn, and ardent appeals to the conscience and the heart, which the Holy Ghost sent down from Heaven, are the only names that are resorted to. These are within the reach of every congregation and every religious community.

"'As to the human activity by which this revival has begun and continues to be extended, it is not through the ministry of the churches alone, or even chiefly. The earnest and faithful preaching of the Word may have been the preparation in some degree, but the chief and honoured agents in the work are the converted themselves. Not through the school of human learning, but taught of God, very many of them have gifts of utterance, and prayer, and exhortation that are powerful instruments for good. Speaking from what they feel, they have a great power in awakening slumbering souls. This group could be multiplied to any extent and in any locality. Their honour and success lie in this – that they are fellow workers with God. Some are mocking still, and throwing a cold and withering indifference on the revival, from which better things might have been expected, and others are ascribing it to the work of Satan, transformed into an angel of light. Let them beware. Let them stand in awe and sin not, lest they be found to fight even against God. We pretend not to understand, or to explain, all the physical effects by which this revival is accompanied. There are mysteries connected with it which are incomprehensible. Still, we cannot believe that it is all the result of mere human approval, or a physical disease, or the result of Satanic work.

"'In the awakening of slumbering souls – their agonising cry for mercy – their repentance and forsaking of favourite sins – their acceptance of Christ – their invitation to Him to sit enthroned on the highest and best seat of their affection – a love to Jesus in their earnest believing prayer – their entrance to new life, and their preserving endeavours to win sinners to the Saviour – we see the grace of God, and are glad. It is truly a time of refreshing from the Lord. Never were our hearts so glad, and our hands so strengthened in the service of God. Oh! May the Lord prolong the gracious season – may He extend it to all our churches, all our localities, and all our families. May ours be the wrestling power of Jacob, that will restrain the Lord to abide with us still, and will not let Him go until He blesses more and more. May the Lord not only give us the drops, but the showers, and the floods promised. The Lord says, 'I will pour water upon him that is thirsty, and floods upon the dry ground: I will pour My Spirit upon thy seed, and My blessing upon thine offspring'.   And we say, 'Remember the word unto Thy servant, upon which thou hast caused me to hope.'"

"The Newsletter" Saturday, 28th May, 1859

The Revival Movement

"Yesterday, according to previous announcements, revival meetings were held in Great George's Street Presbyterian Church, at one o'clock in the afternoon and at eight o'clock in the evening, when the religious services were conducted by two of those recently converted at the meetings in the district around Ballymena. There was an exceedingly large attendance at the evening meeting, the church having become completely filled at the appointed hour and several, who afterwards arrived, were unable to obtain admission. The latter were, however, addressed outside the church by the Rev. John White, Wesleyan Methodist Minister, who took his stand in front of the Rev. Mr. Toye's residence and, after conducting singing and prayer, delivered a very impressive sermon to a congregation numbering upwards on one thousand people.

"The service within the church was opened by a middle-aged man who took his stand on a platform in front of the pulpit and, having conducted religious worship, offered up a most earnest prayer; he then proceeded to address the large audience assembled. In doing so he related his own religious experience, describing the change which had been wrought in his soul through the influence of the Spirit and faith in Christ Jesus; that he had been brought 'from darkness to light, and from the power of Satan unto God'. He then appealed, with great earnestness, to all present, to accept the gift of salvation as he had done, to exercise faith in Christ as the only means of obtaining that salvation, and to become reconciled to God. He then spoke with great ease and in a very pathetic and touching style, which produced, as it was calculated to do, a visible impression on all present.

"After he had concluded, a young man, apparently about twenty years of age, took the place vacated by his companion and continued the religious service. He spoke with the accent of a County Antrim peasant, in good broad Scottish, but with a depth of feeling which told on all who heard him. He demonstrated knowledge of gospel truth, and evangelical Christianity, a zeal for the cause of God, and a desire to be instrumental in bringing others to experience the realities of the gospel which he professed to feel himself. All who heard him seemed deeply impressed with the truths which he enforced with all the earnestness of a youth and new convert.

"In prayer both of these men seemed to possess their greatest strength. They then showed that they were really in earnest. Every sentence was a petition coming from men who appeared to feel that those for whom they prayed wanted something which could be procured through prayer alone. They are to remain in Belfast today, where they will conduct revival meetings in the same place of worship and at the same hours as on yesterday."

"The Ballymena Observer" Saturday, 28th May 1859

"On the evening of Thursday 19th May the public excitement, particularly in Springwell Street, was intense and we visited that locality with the expressed purpose of witnessing, and reporting upon, the phenomena as previously described. On one portion of the street we found a crowd of at least two thousand people, engaged in services of prayer, and praise, under the leadership of laymen. Six or seven houses elsewhere in the same street were crowded with people in every spot where standing room could be obtained. The doors and, in some cases, the windows were open and besieged by a throng of all classes, anxious to hear, or to obtain a glimpse of the proceedings within.

"Having made our way up a narrow staircase, crowded with anxious listeners, we entered a small apartment in which about twenty people, of both sexes, were grouped in various attitudes of deep attention, or silent devotion. A neatly dressed young woman, apparently about twenty two years of age, had been stricken one hour previously, and was supported in the arms of an elderly female who was sitting upon a low stool. Her utterance was a cry and, for some time, rather incoherent; but mingled with sobs and moans, and agonising expressions of despair, we could distinguish exclamations like the following:- 'Is there no hope!', 'Oh, my heart, my heart!', 'Pardon, pardon!', 'Oh Jesus, save me!', 'Oh God, have mercy!' Beside this poor girl two men were standing, and praying aloud alternatively. In other portions of the room we could see that hands were clasped, and that tears were silently streaming from many an eye turned heavenward; but our attention was attracted to the movements of a young woman, evidently of the lower classes, who had been stricken two days previously, but had now recovered and was bending over the sufferer with emotions exhibiting the deepest consideration. She told her of Jesus the Redeemer, Who was ever willing to save. She repeated passages of scripture that spoke of hope and consolation to the repentant, and then burst forth into a lengthy, and apparently impulsive, prayer, well expressed and perfectly intelligent. We noted down some of her expressions at the moment, and they were precisely as follows:- 'Oh Lord Jesus, Saviour of Sinners, look down in mercy upon this awakened soul!' 'Oh give her faith, and strength, and hope!' Blessed and Holy Spirit, give her light!' 'Oh God the Father, God the Redeemer, and the Comforter, bring help and salvation!' After this manner of prayer, occasionally broken with necessary attention to the sufferer, she proceeded for a full fifteen minutes. Now it may be asked, 'Who was this earnest petitioner for peace and consolation to the afflicted sufferer?' The reply can be given in a dozen words that contain matter which would fill volumes. Four days previous to the evening of which we write, she was a reckless, and apparently God-forsaken young woman – a common street prostitute in Ballymena. Before we left the scene which we have thus attempted to describe, the impressed party had obtained considerable relief, and at intervals we observed that her lips were silently moving as if in secret prayer. Our visit to Springwell Street extended over a period of four hours.

"In the meantime, the movement was progressing constantly in every district of the surrounding country. Soon after breakfast hour, on Saturday morning, six or seven young women became suddenly affected with all the usual symptoms, while engaged at work in one of the weaving departments of the spinning factory, at Graceview. Intense excitement immediately ensued among the workers; the alarm soon became general, and within an hour twenty or thirty people of both sexes were found prostrate. The business of the entire establishment was interrupted, and as a matter of necessity, the factory was closed at midday. It was re-opened on Monday, but nearly half the ordinary numbers of hands were found absent, and we understand that a business at Ballygarvey bleach works has been seriously hindered owing to a similar situation.

"About six o'clock, on the evening of Sunday last, a congregation numbering four thousand people of the neighbourhood assembled in the open-air, in front of the Presbyterian Church in Broughshane, where services of prayer and exhortation were conducted by the Rev. Mr. Robinson and by a number of revival converts from other localities. On the same evening open-air prayer meetings were held at Carniney, Cullybackey and Straid. At Carniney, the crowd numbered two thousand and they separated into two large groups, for each of which there was a speaker."

"The Belfast Newsletter" Wednesday, 1ˢᵗ June 1859

The Revival Movement in Belfast

"Every minister of every evangelical denomination in town seems in favour of the movement and identifying with it, with a single exception; namely one Presbyterian minister being, to some extent, opposed to the whole matter. His congregation, which happens not to be either large or influential, is generally treated to a discourse condemning the movement and everything connected with it. At the present time, sectarianism should not be known and, rather than stir up in any way the sectarian spirit, we refrain from naming the individual in question. But, on Sunday last, he let his bigotry and sectarianism so overcome him that, in both his morning and evening sermons, he referred to the union prayer meeting and declared his intention not to be present, as he could not sit on the same platform with ministers of the Anglican Church. The meeting could not display a better spirit than by offering up special prayer on his behalf, that the Spirit Who is at work amongst the people, might touch his heart.

"The union prayer meeting, to be held in the Music Hall at one o'clock today, is expected to be one of the best meetings which has yet assembled in Belfast. The Lord Bishop will preside. A large number of ministers of all denominations will attend and no doubt, the only difficulty will be the want of sufficient space for the public.

"The Banner of Ulster" Thursday, 2nd June 1859

The Religious Awakening in County Antrim

"We are not astonished at the conduct of certain influential people on the judicial bench, or in Unitarian pulpits, who sneer at that remarkable movement in our midst which has begun to monopolise such a large share of public curiosity and attention. An influential person in the Roman Catholic press sneered at the 'fanaticism' of the 'Northern Dissenters', as if the Church of Rome had not become the very by-word for the grossest extravagance. Need we remind our contemporary of the foul mouth utterances of the French preachers of the league, whose obscenities and sanctified trivia were so monstrous that, compared with them, the maddest rant of an American camp meeting would be calm and sensible? But it is not necessary for us to vindicate this movement against such attacks. If it be genuine, it will vindicate itself; if not, it will die out without a stroke from this satirist.

"The most tangible proof of the genuineness of this work is to be found in its remarkable results, as evidenced in the disappearance of vice, the prevalence of a high tone of morality, and the conversion of Roman Catholics, Unitarians and other errorists. Cursing and swearing are not to be heard; drunkenness has almost disappeared; public houses have been closed; family quarrels have been made up; the Sabbath is observed; Arians have joined Trinitarian churches; and Roman Catholics have burned their prayer books, and become Protestants, in spite of all the virtues of holy water and wine. Above all, the converts are not critical, arrogant or accusing, but dwelling together in peace, kindliness and love. These would certainly be strange fruits of spurious revival, and we leave all whom it concerns to explain as they may."

"The Banner of Ulster" Saturday, 4th June 1859

Berry Street Church

"This place of worship has been virtually the centre of the present religious movement in Belfast. On Wednesday evening a meeting was held by a number of gentlemen who have been deeply impressed by the Spirit, through the present awakening. One of the brethren from Ballymena spoke, who has been largely blessed by being made the instrument of the awakening to many souls in his own town and neighbourhood. At the meeting a very decided manifestation, such as that observed in other parts of the county, was visible. One female, unable to restrain her feelings, screamed out and, shortly afterwards, several people, men and women, were similarly affected – about twenty.

"These people were all visited on the following day by many clergymen and others, all of whom speak of the decided change which has been wrought in their character and whole feelings. On Thursday evening another meeting was held in Berry Street Church, which was so largely attended that many hundreds were unable to get admittance; indeed, the doors had to be shut to prevent the enormous pressure from without the building. As on the previous evening, the meeting was conducted by a brother from Ballymena with one of those, we believe, affected by the previous evening, one or two clergymen and others.

"The manifestations at this meeting were somewhat the same as on Wednesday evening, except that the number of those awakened was much larger. At one time the cries from both males and females were so great that the person offering up prayer had to cease and give out a Psalm which, to some extent, soothed their feelings. Several of those awakened were taken home, while others were slowly awakened by their mental agony as to be unfit to be removed 'til a late hour of the night. We have heard of a number of females who had attended the

Wednesday evening meeting, having become affected the next day, during their working hours.

"Yesterday evening the excitement and anxiety to be present during the religious worship were almost indescribable. Half past seven was the hour appointed for the opening of the church, but long before that time, the entire neighbourhood was so densely thronged that the streets became almost impassable. The building would not have contained one-fifth of the number who sought admittance and, when completely filled, it was necessary, for purposes of safety alone, to close the doors. A strong body of the local police was stationed in the vicinity to prevent disorder and annoyance, but very little occurred of this sort. Many of the persons who waited in the street had come there without going home after leaving work.

"On the shutting of the doors the crowd divided into three sections, determined to hold meetings in other churches; these were – May Street, Eglinton Street, and in the Wesleyan Chapel, Donegal Place. The religious services in Berry Street were conducted by the Rev. Hugh Hanna, the Rev. James Wilson and several lay brethren. While they were proceeding, a large number were struck down prostrate, while a great many others were manifestly labouring under a strong conviction of sin. It is worthy of special remark that a majority of those who had been thus impressed since the commencement of these meetings had found hope and peace in Christ, and are now devoting themselves, with extraordinary zeal, to the exhortation of their friends and neighbours to flee to the Saviour.

"Many of them depicting in language, remarkable for its appropriateness, the evil and dangers of sin, as well as the preciousness of Christ, and the attractions and glory of Heaven. On each evening the people have concluded and could scarcely be got to separate, even at a late hour. When the congregation had been dismissed, numbers of them still continued praying on the stairs and in the grounds. Not a few who attended the meetings were overtaken by conviction in their homes and at their employment on the following day. Some of the persons who became affected in the church were carried into the Sexton's house and into the adjacent grounds, where people affectionately prayed over them.

"After the conclusion of the meeting last night the Rev. Messrs. Hanna and Wilson proceeded to visit some of the cases at Ewarts Row and other localities. Rev. Hanna considers that a work, equal in importance to that of a sanctuary, remains to be done in the homes of the people – as an instance of which he mentions that, while he was praying for one, another was struck down. These events have originated a general feeling of seriousness among the mass of the Protestant people of Belfast and belief that we are on the eve of a great outpouring of the Spirit. We shall perhaps be able in our next paper to detail some of the more striking instances in connection with the awakenings in Rev. Hanna's church."

The Crumlin Road

"An intense and very general excitement has prevailed in the factory of Messrs. Ewart & Son, Crumlin Road, and the streets in the immediate vicinity in which many of the workers reside, because a number of the females employed in the mill have exhibited sudden religious impressions, quite as strong as those manifested in any of the meetings where awakenings have occurred. We are informed and have no reason to doubt that more than twenty cases of this description – several of them of the most marked character – have already taken place. The particulars of some of these have been detailed to us and are in almost every respect similar to other instances of deep and absorbing spiritual impression which we have witnessed, heard or read of.

"On some occasions the persons affected have become utterly prostrated under the visitation and so incapacitated from the slightest physical exertion that they required to be conveyed to their homes and placed under medical treatment. From this state most of them recovered within a few hours, but still obtain a deep conviction of the urgent necessity of saving grace. Others have been enabled to rejoice in the presence of a revealed Saviour and one prominent and general feature is their ardent affection for those who are convicted, or whom they desire to be convicted in the same manner. For the conversion of their relatives and companions their prayers are frequent and incessant. Some of them now enjoy perfect peace of mind and are constant in their efforts to awaken or console others.

"This is shown by two young females who were struck down in Messrs. Ewart's Mill on Thursday morning and whose cases excited a profound sensation among their fellow workers. The females convicted had not previously attended any of the recent meetings for prayer, or to hear religious messages and it is remarkable that, although they worship in various congregations, the majority when in their calmer stage of spiritual fervour expressed an earnest desire to be visited by a particular minister (the Rev. Hugh Hanna) who has since been most diligent in his attention to them, even proceeding to their houses for the purpose of prayer and advice, after a long evening's pastoral labour. An entire change seems to have taken place, not only in the hearts of many who are affected, but also in the enlargement of their intellectual powers and their capacity for clothing their thoughts and wishes in language which surprises them, as well as their hearers' hearts.

"We learned that the females, who have been the subject of this wonderful visitation, have been treated with the kindest consideration by the proprietors and managers of the establishment, in which they are employed – and that, when some of those who were most powerfully stricken were removed to their homes, others united in prayer for them."

Meetings in York Street Church

"This meeting had not been announced in any pulpits on last Sabbath except York Street, neither had notice of it been given in any newspaper yet, before the hour of the meeting on Thursday evening, the church was crowded in every part. Precisely at half past seven, the appointed hour, the Rev. Mr. Hamilton and Messrs. McQuilken and Meneely, two members of the church at Connor, entered the pulpit. Mr. Hamilton stated to the congregation that it was evident that many of those who desired to join in the religious worship of the evening, could not be accommodated in the church.

"Thus, it was the garden at the rear of the church which was opened, and one of the friends from Connor addressed those who could assemble there. The immense crowds in front of the church immediately entered the garden, which had been covered with forms from the school rooms and by the young men of the church. The meeting in the open-air which occupied nearly the entire large garden, the property of the congregation, was opened with praise and prayer by one of the elders. Mr. Hamilton, having opened the meeting in the church by singing the 126th Psalm and by prayer, said that the meeting would be addressed by two members of the church of Connor – a church in which he had laboured for the first ten years of his ministry – a church which was very dear to him. He had known these friends when they were children, and rejoiced to see them in his present congregation telling the works of God, where he had first ministered the Word of life.

"One of them had given himself to the Lord about two years before. When he heard 'the Spirit and the Bride say, 'Come,'' he sought to obey the Divine command by saying to others 'Come.' He taught at a Sabbath School class. The Lord gave him another young man of like spirit to be a fellow labourer. They met for prayer. Another joined them, and another, and another. They prayed for the Sabbath School classes – that the Lord would bless the Word for the salvation of the children. They had not long continued in this exercise 'til they saw their prayers answered in one and another of their scholars. This encouraged them greatly. They increased their labours and their numbers increased until, while they wished not to be seen, their work grew up into public notice.

"The addresses were full of solid gospel truth, with much unction and delivered with much earnestness – nothing flimsy and nothing to awaken mere feeling. They were highly Calvinist – humbling to the sinner and glorifying to the Saviour. Mr. Hamilton announced that there would be a meeting for prayer in the lower school room of the church, the next morning at half past seven where there had been a meeting at the same time on the previous morning. He stated that there had been a prayer meeting in the school room by young men of the congregation for a considerable time, and another held by the elders in the session room every Saturday evening. It was gratifying to him that both of these meetings had begun, and carried on, without any suggestion on his part, but rather entirely by the elders and young men themselves. After singing and prayer, the immense congregation separated at twenty minutes past nine."

"The Ballymena Observer" Saturday, 4ᵗʰ June 1859

"The Rev. Daniel Mooney, of this parish, has been distinguished by the earnest labour in the guidance, and consolation, of the 'convicted'. At the close of an excellent sermon, during the morning service of the church last Sunday, he addressed the congregation as follows:— 'I do not intend, on the present occasion, to enter into any discussion on the merits of this most remarkable religious movement, or to supply you with any description of its peculiar phases, or details of its working, as I propose with God's blessing to make it the subject of next Sunday's discourse; but I cannot refrain saying this much at present, that for what I have seen of it, it is my deliberate opinion that it is a real work, a great work, a necessary work, a glorious work – a work that must be ascribed to the Spirit of God.

"'I am not lightly or hastily come to this conclusion; I pronounced no judgement until I examined the matter most carefully myself; and I now solemnly declare that the evidence has been so irresistible, it is impossible to shut my eyes against the truth. I believe it to be one of those times of refreshment, spoken of by the Apostle, which were to come from the presence of the Lord. I believe it to be an outpouring of the Spirit, though not on so grand a scale as on the Day of Pentecost, when the fiery tongues descended and miraculous powers were given – yet such a one as suited to the times and adequate to the accomplishment of God's purposes. On the Day of Pentecost, the establishment of Christianity was the great object to be accomplished. In the days of the reformation, gospel truth had to be replaced on the lofty prominence from whence it had been thrown down by falsehood and error – that was the great object of the reformation.

"'Now if we may venture to interpret the mind of the Spirit, the great work that is in the hands seems to be the replacement of practical religion in the place of the deadness, formality and empty profession, which pressed down like a nightmare upon the spirit of Christianity. It is not that the gospel truth was hidden under a bushel – it was not that the gospel light did not shed its rays abundantly – it was not that the true doctrines of Christianity were not preached almost everywhere – it was not that they were not understood by most of the people.

"'No, I believe there never was a period when knowledge so abounded – cheap religious publications, the distribution of the Bible, the multiplication of Sunday Schools, and the traditional preaching of our pulpits, with few exceptions, conveyed to the minds of the people such an amount of religious knowledge as never before existed in this country. But that seemed to be all – they all seemed to rest. Heartfelt reception of the blessed truths of the gospel seemed to be as far distant as when they were buried under the rubbish of Romanist errors and superstitions. Who was the better for what he heard? Who became a devoted servant of Jesus, and a soldier of the Cross? Who followed His steps, who copied His example, who despised the world, and set his affections on things above? Who, when told that in order to come to Christ he must be convicted of sin, felt convicted? Who, when he was called to repent, did repent and forsake his sins? Who, when the wrath of God was preached against sinners, felt the least alarmed? Did not people come to the House of God, and hear those things spoken of, and go through their prayers, and return back again to their homes just as they came? Have not these been permanently the days of lifeless profession, of deadness and formality; and how needful then that the good Spirit of God, through Jesus, should send a time of refreshment to water the withered, and dying souls of mere nominal and formal Christians.'

"The Rev. John McNaughton shared, with his church, a visit to Ballymena. He commenced that he had heard so much of the work that was going on at Ballymena. He felt that it was his duty to go there and see for himself what the state of things was, and to form a judgement, so far as he could, on what he saw and heard of the character of that very remarkable movement.

"There were some things about it that he did not pretend to understand – he did not see his way yet thoroughly to understand them; but there were other things about which a way-faring man, though a fool, could not err – which are the actual and obvious results of the movement. It was impossible to be mistaken of the fact that drunkenness has altogether disappeared; that public houses have been closed every week; that in some districts which he himself had visited, and which were formerly characterised by profane swearing, such a thing as an oath, or a curse, was not to be heard.

"He found that families, who had always refused to speak together on the account of family or property quarrels, had been reconciled and people were living in peace with each other, taking part in private and public worship. These were the effects of the work; whatever might be the cause of them was another question, but they were blessed results and he wished they were seen over the length and breadth of the land. They were not things to be sneered at, or made a subject of rudeness and joking. They were not likely to be the results of the devil's work. That was not the way in which Beelzebub supports his kingdom. There was another fact very apparent – there is a general feeling of seriousness pervading the entire population.

"Mr. McNaughton then mentioned that he called on one of the ministers of Ballymena, and told him what the object of his mission was, and he asked him to give direction to some people who were under religious conviction. They then went out and came to the end of a lane, which answers to some of the streets in the neighbourhood of Talbot Street, or North Queen Street, and the barracks, in that town – in fact, the haunts of the outcasts in that town. Mr. Dill then said to him, 'I think you should preach here.' He said, in reply, 'There is no one to hear me but yourself, and that would be a small congregation, but tell the people in some of the homes that there is to be a sermon here and bring some of them out.' 'That is not necessary', he said; 'Just let me open a Bible and give out a Psalm.' Certainly something new.

"He opened the Bible and the first line was hardly sung until one door opened and a person ran across the street with a chair. By and by door after door opened, and people looked out, and before they had two verses sung, the people were crowding together. The audience was composed almost altogether of people from that neighbourhood. Thousands passing along the streets, some of them from the better ranks of life, remained and joined in the singing as they stood.

"In fact he never preached to a more attentive congregation in his life, and many of the poor creatures were bathed in tears, not because of the things he was saying, for he avoided what was moving or stirring, but he wanted to see what would be the result of a simple declaration of the gospel truth. They were dismissed in a most orderly way, and he spoke to one or two of them. One person was very much influenced in particular, which had been evident from her appearance leading a very different kind of life. 'Do you feel', said he, 'some concern about your soul's salvation?' She replied, with a smile, that she was past that, and that she had found Christ. They then went to the church – it was past seven o'clock and the church was very near full with a large congregation of all classes. Poor people were sitting side by side with well dressed people."

Ahoghill

"One of the most remarkable character changes yet on record occurred at Ahoghill on Sunday 22nd May. The object of visitation was a boy of that neighbourhood, well known as one of the most wicked and unrestrained characters that had ever troubled a community – a public nuisance in fact – a wretched outcast, whose heart was habitually filled with malice towards man, and whose mouth was filled with blasphemy towards God. He had never seriously attended a religious service, of any description, in the whole course of his existence. He was a mocker of all prayer, and delighted in imitating the revivalists.

"On the Sunday referred to, whilst a congregation of Presbyterians were assembling for public worship, he stationed himself near the entrance of the church, and there, in language of the grossest obscenity, he annoyed, reviled, and cursed, the passing people. After some of them he shouted, 'Ah, ah! The devil will get hold of you today!' To others he cried, 'Run fast or you will get the touch!'

"Now, we state a fact well known to hundreds of the population when we say that within one hour, and long before the separation of the assembled worshippers, the wicked boy was struck to the earth with a thunderbolt! He fell prostrate and senseless upon the very scene of his iniquity! It was, at first, supposed that he had been summoned to final retribution at the bar of the All-powerful – but the visitation was 'in mercy and not judgement'. Speech was restored, and with it came the soul piercing stings of an awakened conscience. His despair was exhibited in words, and gestures, too horrible for description. He writhed in mental agonies for which the imaginative can find no parallel, except in the endless torments of the eternally lost. We pause, not over the long protracted struggle, the crisis, the awakening hope, or the impulsive supplication for Heaven's mercy; but over the fact, be it explained as it may – that, in the course of the following week, this soul smitten sinner, weak in body and thoroughly subdued in spirit, was found crawling to every prayer meeting in the neighbourhood beseeching others to pray for him, and praying most humbly and earnestly for himself."

"The Newsletter" Monday, 6th June 1859

"Meetings for prayer and exhortation are being held daily. Sinners are being convicted of their exceeding sinfulness in the sight of God, and souls are being converted – made happy in the pardoning love of God – renewed in righteousness and truthfulness – made heirs of God, and joint-heirs with Christ. There is an evidence of the outpouring of God in answer to believing, faithful prayer. The most sceptical who will but attend one of the meetings, now held in any of the churches or other places at this time will be compelled to admit that the Hand of the Lord is visibly at work, and that His blessing attends the means used for bringing sinners to seek happiness in the Saviour's love. All evangelical denominations have joined in this good work and success – marvellous.

"Each Protestant place of worship in this town is becoming rapidly filled. There are no empty pews now – no unoccupied seats. Every evening the streets are crowded with hundreds and thousands who are wending their way – not to the place of amusement – not to join in the giddy dance – not to attend either theatre or concert – but with their Bibles, Hymn books and Psalm books in their hands, eagerly pressing onward to the House of God, to endeavour to obtain admission in time so that they may therein hear instruction as to how they should escape from the city of destruction and, at length, reach the Celestial Kingdom. At the services conducted in the different churches many have been led to seek pardon, and many professed to have obtained it and are now going on their way rejoicing. It was considered by some that a union prayer meeting, in which all evangelical denominations might unite, should be held, and accordingly steps were taken for holding it."

A Prayer Meeting in the Wellington Hall

"On Saturday evening, as previously announced in "The Newsletter", a union prayer meeting was held in the Wellington Hall at eight o'clock when a large number, chiefly men, attended. It was to be regretted however that, although ministers of all denominations were invited and requested to attend, they did not do so; none of the ministers of the town being present that we could observe, with the exception of the Rev. William Anderson, Curate of the Parish. This may be accounted for, perhaps by the fact that they were almost all engaged either at other large meetings, or in visiting those who have repented in their respective residences."

The Religious Revival in Belfast

"The meeting was presided over by Alderman Hamilton, and was opened with singing and prayer conducted by Mr. George Smith. The Chairman then read the portion of the Acts of the Apostles that records the extraordinary work of revival that took place in Jerusalem on the Day of Pentecost in answer, no doubt, to the fervent prayer of the one hundred and twenty disciples who had been 'all with one accord in one place'. Having made a few practical observations on this account of the first religious revival in connection with Christianity, singing and prayer were engaged in, at intervals, by the laymen present, and a deep and solemn feeling seemed to overcome the entire assembly. At the close of the meeting it was arranged that a similar service should be conducted in the same place at seven o'clock tomorrow (Tuesday morning) and again next Saturday evening."

Falls Road Church

"A special prayer meeting was held in the Falls Road Wesleyan Church on Saturday evening. Nearly all present were led to seek the Lord with sighs and tears, and one of the most remarkable movements yet experienced in connection with this revival took place. There appeared to be none who were not convicted in the meeting. Those who had, in years gone by, been made happy were engaged in advising the convicted, pointing them to 'the Lamb of

God, which taketh away the sin of the world', praying with them and for them, exhorting them to exercise simple faith, and many departed knowing that 'There is therefore now no condemnation to them which are in Christ Jesus'."

Salem Church

"At the services in Salem (Methodist) Church, York Street, yesterday morning and evening, the work of revival was also witnessed. The Rev. Mr. Graham preached appropriate sermons on each occasion, and with blessed results. At two o'clock in the afternoon he held a prayer meeting in the house of one of the members of the congregation in Hardinge Street; several became convicted, and some of them departed for their homes justified through faith in Jesus. After the evening service Mr. Graham conducted a revival prayer meeting when many were convicted of sin. Benches were placed for the convicted to go forward and kneel at, in order that special prayer might be offered up on their behalf. A large number cast aside all shame and, having left their seats, knelt at the repentance benches. A few of the class leaders advised those, thus under conviction of sin, to direct their minds to the Saviour, and pointed out to them the way in which to obtain mercy.

"Suitable hymns were sung, different laymen present offered up prayer, especially for the convicted, and the result was that some of them, through faith, obtained pardon and left rejoicing in God their Saviour. It was announced that special revival prayer meetings would be held every evening during the present week, in one of the school rooms attached to the church, so that the work, now commenced, may be carried on.

"The work of revival is thus going on extensively in Belfast. In some districts of the town the entire inhabitants of not a few of the streets have been up throughout the night engaged in prayer with, and for, each other. Those who hardly ever prayed before are now doing so and a change in their lives, walk and conversation has been affected. Long neglected Bibles are being dusted and carefully read, family prayer has been commenced in their homes; in short, hundreds are becoming real and sincere Christians. The work of God is being helped forward on all sides, prayer meetings are held daily in almost every street, and souls are becoming converted at these services conducted solely by laymen. The deepest interest is taken in the movement by almost all classes, and those who would throw any obstacle in the way of its progress are but a very small minority of the community."

"The Belfast Telegraph" Tuesday, 7th June 1859

The Religious Revival in Belfast

"The religious revival in Belfast, its vicinity, and indeed throughout County Antrim, as well as adjoining counties, still continues to spread. The work is so extensive in its character, the numbers convicted of sin are so numerous, the souls pardoned are so many, that it is wholly impossible to convey any adequate idea of what is, in reality, occurring. In Belfast, in almost every street, there are numbers of converts, and in every family some soul professes salvation. Roman Catholics have come under its influence, and even degraded outcasts on the street have repented, although they have not been attending the religious meetings in any of the churches. In not a few instances, whole families have been led to seek salvation, and now rejoice in the enjoyment of pardoning love.

"Ministers of all denominations, as well as laymen, are daily engaged in going from house to house visiting, advising and praying with new converts, and hundreds who have retired from the churches in deep agony of mind, have subsequently been made happy while engaged in prayer and exercise of faith in their own homes. Strong minded men, women of tender and susceptible feelings, sceptics who laughed at the truths of religion, scoffers who went to mock have been all affected by the movement and, in many instances, the mental suffering and consequent weakness of body in the cases of hard, able and robust sons of toil, have been most extraordinary, and the joy of these, on having their burden of sin rolled off at the foot of the Cross, has been most intense. Countenances that a moment before were sad, downcast and wet with tears, instantly became lightened up with joy, proceeding from the newly imparted feeling communicated when they became reconciled to God.

"In some cases, ministers of religion from their pulpits declared that they have, themselves, been blessed by the present revivals; that they never knew how to preach the gospel in all its fullness before; that the simple gospel, and not controversy, was what ought to be proclaimed to their congregations and that, in the future, they were determined to preach nothing but 'Jesus Christ and Him Crucified'. It is remarkable too, in connection with the revival meetings, that in churches where no member of the congregation ever needed a prayer, they now bow their knees in humility at the Throne of Grace, while cries are heard, from every part of the assembly, of – 'God be merciful to me a sinner'.

"The meetings in several churches continue to be held each evening, and the attendance is so large that room cannot be found for many of those anxious to be present."

Berry Street Church

"Last evening, a meeting was held, as usual, in Berry Street Church, and so great was the rush of those desirous of being present that every available seat was occupied before seven o'clock, at which hour it was found necessary to close the doors and gates so that the service might be conducted without interruption. Religious worship, similar to that carried on at former meetings, was engaged in, when laymen chiefly offered up prayer with great earnestness. Many became convicted of sin and, in some cases, physical prostration was the result, while others were soon enabled to rejoice that they had experienced the new birth, without the personal realisation of which, as taught by the Saviour, that no man shall 'see the Kingdom of God'.

"When the services had been conducted for some time the doors were opened, and part of the congregation had no sooner left than their places were taken by others – the meeting having thus to be continued until a late hour. Much good was evidently effected at this, as at former meetings of a similar character, and numbers are being daily led from a course of sin to a life of righteousness.

"Such is a slight view of the manner in which the revival movement is proceeding in Belfast. To give an account of the many instances connected with it would be beyond the limits of a newspaper. Each street, almost each house, furnishes details of an extensive and interesting character. In one family the daughters have been brought to know their sins forgiven; they spoke of the joy they felt to their parents and brothers, entreating them to be also 'reconciled to God'. Conviction seized these and soon the whole family found peace and were made members of the family in Heaven – members by adoption and grace. A minister cannot pass through a street but he is asked to visit some convicted person, and many of the cases which come thus under their notice are most remarkable and touching.

"Last evening, a minister, in passing the vicinity of Market Street, was requested to visit a female then under conviction. He, at once, yielded to the request and was taken through narrow lanes until, at length, he reached a miserable residence, in which there was neither furniture nor scarcely bedding. The convicted woman lay on a bed of straw, in great agony of mind. The Rev. Gentleman, having enquired what her real state was, spoke words of consolation to her and prayed with her. She soon found peace through faith in the atonement of the world's Saviour and, although her earthly home afforded little comfort, she was enabled to rejoice that she could lay claim to an inheritance 'incorruptible, and undefiled' – to a 'mansion' in her Father's House above.

"Another interesting case of conversion has come to our knowledge. A whole family, consisting of five persons, has been brought under the influence of the Spirit's working. The mother – the head of the household – had long since been reconciled to God, but her children had not given themselves up to Christ. In the family was a young man of great promise as regards worldly concerns, but careless and indifferent about his soul's eternal welfare. He saw his sisters, one after another, brought to a sense of guilt and to conversion through

Christ, the change being accompanied with the usual extraordinary mental and physical sufferings, but he remained unchanged, and still expressed his doubts as to the reality of the work.

"At length, he began to think. He saw his whole family professing peace and joy in their Saviour, and manifesting great concern for his conversion. The question suggested itself with a terrible force to his mind – 'Are they all saved, and shall I be lost forever?' He betook himself at once to a private apartment, there to pray. He soon felt the enormity of his guilt; he cried out in agony for mercy and pardon, through the righteousness of the Redeemer, and was blessed in finding peace such as the world cannot give and cannot take away. He has since been in a state of great physical weakness, but strong in the Lord and rejoicing in the great work wrought in his soul. This is one of many similar cases occurring in our town, almost every hour, and shows the reality of the revival work.

"Several Roman Catholics have also been convicted and consequently brought to a saving knowledge of Christ crucified, instead of a knowledge of a crucifix. In some instances, the Priests have been called in to visit them, but no sooner did their 'Reverences' hear the expressions of the convicted, and the prayers of other converts, that they, at once, fled without offering any consolation to the individual under conviction.

Larne

"At Larne, the revival has commenced in real earnest. Last Sunday evening the different places of worship were crowded to excess; many were convicted and converted, and the deepest interest in the movement seems to be felt by all classes of the community. The town is in a state of considerable excitement regarding the matter. Nothing else is talked of, and each individual appears anxious that it should go on and prosper in that district."

"The Banner of Ulster" Tuesday, 7th June 1859

Brown Street District

"Revival meetings have been held in the Brown Street schoolhouse during the whole of last week, with the best results. The attendance, however, became so crowded that the building was unfit to accommodate the numbers who sought admission. The use of Townsend Street Church was requested and, at once, granted and the meetings have since been held there. On Saturday morning, at the unusually early hour of five o'clock, a prayer meeting was held which was largely attended by people of the working class who had left their beds an hour before the accustomed time in order to hear what they might of the good work that is going on. Some of them – indeed a considerable number – manifested a deep earnestness in the proceedings and, when they closed, proceeded to their daily occupations solemnised by the worship of the morning.

"Another prayer meeting was held on Saturday evening and the audience was, again, very large. The interest taken in the proceedings was very deep. No public manifestations of conviction or impression took place while the town missionary, who conducted them, was present. But, after he had retired, one or two cases of this kind occurred, and subsequently a good many more, in the dwellings of people who had listened to the exhortation of the evening. Some of these cases were so serious in character that Christian brethren gave their hearty sympathy towards them and visited the houses of many of the people affected, praying and exhorting until a late hour of the night, with the effects which we have heard described as exceedingly favourable.

"Some of the exhorters were out of bed until three or four o'clock the following morning. On the Sabbath the manifestations were fully as marked and numerous as they had been upon any previous occasion that took place, in most instances, in private houses. A good number of those who were brought under the influence of the Holy Spirit seemed to have been expecting some visitation of this kind for a length of time past. Yesterday a man who was employed as a labourer in an establishment in town became so seriously affected under the effect of awakened feelings that it was found necessary to convey him to his own residence. A Christian gentleman was promptly sent for, who as promptly attended to his spiritual requirements. We are assured upon authority that, in this thickly populated district of Belfast, the work of conviction and conversion is progressing with a rapidity, perfectly amazing."

Ahoghill

"We have received the following interesting letter from the Rev. David Adams, Ahoghill:–

"'My Dear Sir – your excellent paper is very useful in these times of refreshing. I therefore send you the following statement regarding Ahoghill where the 'streams in the desert' first overflowed so abundantly. Here the work of the Lord still advances rapidly and powerfully. Even the profane cease to scoff. Many of them begin to admire and adore, and the people of God can truly say:– 'Then was our mouth filled with laughter, and our tongue with singing'.

"'The Lord was again manifestly present in my church last Sabbath (29th) when, during public worship, upwards of twenty were almost instantaneously impressed with deep religious feelings, just as I have formerly described, while the entire congregation amounting to one thousand two hundred seemed to feel an indescribable emotion – in some awe, in many love. One person told me afterwards that 'Jesus never appeared so lovely to the soul as on that occasion.' On the following Monday evening, our usual weekly prayer meeting in my church was attended by upwards of one thousand and several were much influenced by the Spirit of God. A middle-aged man told me that he never took hold of his Saviour until that night. For even a short time previously, when asked to pray for a convert, his conscience smote him as he was utterly unfit for the task. I conducted the meeting as usual, and prayers were offered and exhortations given by several devout laymen.

"'One of them was Councillor Moore, who has been greatly blessed in his unwearied and self-denying evangelistic labours, and another was a converted Roman Catholic who has, during the last two months, made astonishing progress in the knowledge and practice of gospel truth, as evidenced by his godly demeanour, and by his scripturally earnest prayers and addresses, while often have I heard him read Psalms to the impressed with a tone of glowing love. At the meeting there was also another Roman Catholic convert, a married woman, who had probably never been in a Presbyterian church and who, up to the previous Friday, was a bigoted papist. On that night she was spiritually influenced though she could not read the Bible and was not at any of the revival meetings but, doubtless, she had received, in some way, a little knowledge of the truth. On Saturday, while still under conviction, she refused to send for the Priest, though some of her Presbyterian neighbours in the most liberal manner offered to go for him. She desired a visit from me instead. When I went I found her most anxious with eyes raised to Heaven and clasped hands extended towards the Lord, praying, 'O Lord, pour out Thy Holy Spirit upon my poor soul! O pardon all my sins and fit me for glory.' I called to see her on Tuesday and she was busy learning a lesson from the Bible taught by one of her godly neighbours.

"'The young man, the mocker, whose wonderful conversion near my church, on Sabbath 22nd, I formerly noticed in your paper, seemed indeed to have passed from death unto life and is now regularly attending my Sabbath School and prayer meetings. I had two other prayer meetings this week in the open-air attended by many hundreds and several were enlightened. We now frequently hear men sing Psalms at their daily toil. When visiting yesterday, I passed a carrier who was humming a Divine Song, and I never felt more happy than when I heard the other evening near midnight on the streets of Ahoghill voices chanting the glorious old tune of 'Martyrdom'. It was a heavenly serenade.'"

Ballyclare

"The following private letter contains some matters of interest in relation to religious movements at Ballyclare, Ballynure and the neighbouring districts:–

"'We went to Ballyclare last Thursday night to attend a revival prayer meeting and truly I cannot understand it. I can only say and feel that it was the Lord's doing and marvellous in our eyes. The scene when we arrived baffles all description. Imagine a large meadow, with an immense multitude of people in all attitudes – some praying, weeping and crying for mercy, others lying in utter helplessness only able to utter feebly their entreaties for pardon, surrounded by groups of friends and strangers all interceding for them and urging them on to call on Christ and, again, others with their faces gleaming with a more than earthly light, listening to the speaker with rapture or eyes raised, eloquently praising God with fathers, sons, mothers, daughters, tender children and strong men, the infants of a few years and the grey-haired women, all equally struck, all equally earnest and eloquent.

"'I saw stalwart men led away as if they were helpless children. During the singing of one of the Psalms the voice of praise was ascending in the still evening air, when there was nothing of an exciting tendency being said, a man beside us suddenly burst out into the most terrific cries, running round and round in circles in such a wild manner that it was dangerous to be in his way – when his cries changed suddenly into calls on the Name of Jesus and, in a few minutes after the most awful suffering, he fell unable to stand or even speak. The public houses are empty all through the town. There is a prayer meeting in almost every second house. Groups about the streets are praying or conversing on the all engrossing topic. Public works are stopped in consequence of these strange and awful manifestations of Jehovah's might. All places, all hours are alike, people are struck down while following their daily vocations, or resting on their beds, crossing the fields or transversing the streets – all are alike and all characters are converted instantly.

"'I cannot pretend to give you any accurate account of it. Words cannot describe the thrilling scene we witnessed yesterday evening. There will be a meeting at Ballynure this Friday evening and one here DV on the Sabbath. The most wonderful feature of all this is that there is no enthusiasm or excitement. Among the people the visitation is sudden. The person is removed to a distance by those around but, beyond a mere mention of the name by those who know it, there is no curiosity or wonder manifested and from being one of the wildest towns in the neighbourhood, Ballyclare has become one of the most religious.'"

Ballymoney

"Most of those affected were young girls, but the awakening has spread with so much rapidity that there are now, or were on Wednesday evening, between forty and fifty 'enlightened' as they call it in Ballymoney. One young lad, about fourteen years of age, who has previously, and up to the day of his conversion, been one of the most uncared for lads, who imagined everyone an enemy and who is an enemy to everyone, was one of those affected on Monday night. He went to scoff and exhibited that tendency to many who saw him going to the meeting. But he was brought home making agonising attempts to pray and being tormented with the terrible pangs of a thoroughly awakened conscience. It was not until Wednesday morning that he found peace in believing. He is now rejoicing in assured confidence. There is one peculiarity attached to all who have been enlightened. That is, that they seem only happy in each other's company, and it is no uncommon thing to see ten or a dozen, of those who have found peace, meeting together to visit a 'sister' who has been, like themselves, brought to conviction.

"We, ourselves, saw a lot of these young girls – the girl whom we left so weak that she was unable, half an hour previously, to leave her bed, among the others – with Bibles in their hands, going down the street on a visit of this nature. They have a reverence for God's Word and delight to meet in prayer. Even the most degraded class in the community, those who are called 'unfortunates', have furnished in Ballymoney a convert to a life of purity and peace. We have no hesitation in saying that the revival, so far from being as some have said, the 'result of the influence of the evil one', is an agency welded by a Power Who 'hath done all things well.'"

Interesting Incidents in the Revival

"In Mary's Lane, off Stanley Street, a most remarkable evidence of religious revival has occurred in one family. Five members of the family were struck down on Sunday and they were shortly afterwards attended by some of the clergymen belonging to the adjoining neighbourhood. During the evening three of them found peace and yesterday the entire five expressed their faith and joy in Christ. In other parts of the same lane, equally strange events have taken place. While a member of one of the leading congregations was praying over the bed of one of the affected, a woman fell down before him and began to confess her sins in most troubled tones.

"In another case, while the same person was about to enter a house in the lane, a woman dropped upon her knees before him and, in a torrent of words, called upon the Redeemer to pardon her sin and, in the same lane, three other houses had their converts while prayer was being held. To each of the people the utmost attention was given and words of comfort expressed, so that, when the late hour at night had arrived, nearly all the people who had been visited were able, themselves, to take a leading part in the work of prayer which was going on.

"We have been informed by a person who passed through the locality late on that night, that his attention was called to a house in which a person was praying in a most emphatic and fervent manner. He passed over to the door of the house and discovered that one of the converted – a boy about sixteen years old – was lamenting over his past transgressions and imploring the Saviour's forgiveness for himself. We are told that the language implored by this boy was most eloquent and emotive. At the conclusion of the prayer, a woman fell down in front of the door, affected in the same manner as the other cases which we have already described. She was conveyed to her own home and received the spiritual treatment which her state required."

"The Derry Sentinel" Wednesday, 8th June 1859

"We learn that revival services are to be held in Londonderry on Sunday next – two in East Wall Methodist Chapel and one on the Quay. Several ministers are to attend, as well as some of the newly awakened individuals from Ballymoney.

"We add an interesting communication relative to revival proceedings at Portrush. The union there of ministers of different Protestant denominations was most pleasing and we hope that similar union will be manifested here:–

"'Portrush – on Monday evening the 6th we had a meeting here on the hill overlooking the harbour at half six. There could not have been fewer on the ground than three thousand people. The assembly was addressed by the Rev. Mr. Chichester and the Rev. Mr. Elliott, the Rev. J. Simpson and several laymen who are converts from Ballymoney. Many other clergymen were present. I need not attempt to describe the scene which followed. I never saw such manifestations of God's power – one prostrated here and another there. I think there were upwards of twenty cases. The convicted ones appeared like people in a swoon. The time of their recovery varied. Some an hour or two, and others more. When they spoke they cried out for mercy, and in every instance found peace in believing through the blood of the atonement. What a meeting! Some exhorting you to flee from the wrath to come, others singing Psalms, mingled with shrieks for mercy and the voice of the preacher pointing to the Lamb of God. On the whole, impressions must have been made even on those not convicted, never to be forgotten. When I left at eleven o'clock the Rev. Mr. Chichester, the Rev. Jonathon Simpson, the Rev. Mr. Elliott and others were as actively employed as at the beginning, ministering to the wants of the convicted ones. A meeting was held in Coleraine last night, with similar results. We are to have one in Portstewart on Monday the 13th at half six. The converts are not confined to any sect or class."

"The Newsletter" Wednesday, 8th June 1859

"The religious revival movement in Belfast continues to spread, as being extended to all parts of the town, even in the localities inhabited by the most debased and degraded. The cases of conviction are becoming more frequent in the different factories and work rooms of the town, and in its vicinity. The number of the contrite increases, just as the number of converts amongst their acquaintances and families has increased who, on having found peace with God themselves, have ceased not to proclaim their joy to all around them. Yesterday a number of the workers in the York Street Mill, chiefly females, became convicted and were conveyed to their homes. When ministers and praying friends were called in to advise and pray with them, some of these professed to have experienced pardon and are now rejoicing in the Lord Who has done for them great things.

"A girl, who had been working in one of the warerooms, was yesterday afternoon seized with conviction and, on being taken home, she begged them to send for her minister. This was accordingly done. A layman engaged in prayer with her and after prayer, while singing a verse of a hymn, she became happy and, with joy beaming in her countenance, told them her soul had been set at liberty, and that her sins which were many were all forgiven. Just at this moment her minister entered, and her demonstrations of joy were remarkable. She grasped him by the hands and said, 'Oh, I know now that Jesus is my Saviour. I know He died for me. I know He loves me.' As the Rev. Gentleman was about to depart, she said, 'I will attend the prayer meetings and other meetings regularly for the future. I will not be absent any more.'

"It is remarkable too that the new converts, in their love for the Saviour, and their desire to extend His Kingdom, have shown great generosity in financial matters. An instance of this occurred last evening. After the Rev. John Graham had conducted a class meeting, one of the weekly services, a young woman, who had been converted on Sunday, handed him a generous subscription towards their foreign missions. This is showing, by works, that the conversions are real.

"These revivals form almost the sole topic of conversation amongst all classes throughout Belfast, and its neighbourhood. An erroneous notion seems to prevail regarding the state of those under conviction. It is a prevalent opinion that the convicted who, in many instances, appear weak in body are suffering physically. Now this idea can be at once eliminated by asking any of those who are now rejoicing in the knowledge of God's favour if they felt any bodily pain whatever. It will be found that nothing like physical pain has been endured. The body may have, and undoubtedly has, become apparently weak, but this has been merely the consequences of mental suffering. The convicted in most cases say, 'There is a weight' about their hearts. A weight of the consciousness of sin but bodily they do not suffer. This must be evident to anyone who has observed that, as soon as the mind is set free, the converted person shows no signs of physical suffering.

"The instances, in which those in the mills are seemingly suddenly affected, is also worthy of remark. If these individuals are enquired of, it will be found that their convictions have not been as sudden as would appear. Most of them, if not all, have been suffering mental agony for days, although proceeding with their work and, at length, the anguish of their minds having reached a climax, they can no longer continue their labours. They have heard a word of exhortation, or a message, from some acquaintance, or in some church and this, having taken hold upon their minds, they think it over and try perhaps to forget it – but find it returning and, after experiencing this for days, they ultimately yield and embrace salvation.

"In the country districts the revivals are extending, and the influence of this movement will, in all probability, be felt the length and breadth of the land."

"The Banner of Ulster" Thursday, 9th June 1859

The Spinning Mills

"One of the most extraordinary features of the awakening from its very commencement has been its almost electric spread among the female workers, not in one particular factory at a time but in several mills simultaneously and, in all, with precisely the same results. That conviction of sin should, at once, have seized upon and stricken down numbers in a day and even in an hour, among that special class of workers, is all but miraculous, and a large proportion of them were known to treat serious matters and persons in a spirit of the utmost levity. The leavening of reviving grace among them, however, has been of a deeply permeating character and has already produced the most serious, spiritual and moral results.

"Many who, without previously exhibiting any signs of impression, were prostrated in a moment under feelings they had never before experienced, are hopeful subjects of redeeming mercy – changed in heart, in manner, in walk and conversation. Those who rarely, if ever, had visited a church or a prayer meeting, are now found regularly and anxiously joining in the religious worship in both, and bearing to their homes and their neighbourhoods the glad tidings of great joy which they hear from time to time. We have been informed of several young women, mill workers, who were in the practice of spending their evenings and Sabbaths in frivolous amusements, now devoting their leisure hours on both to hearing of God and Christ in prayer and in holy communion with each other.

"We have already told of the almost unparalleled visitation which occurred in Messrs. Ewart's Mill, Crumlin Road, last week, and the far pervading influence which it exercised and in which it is still producing its natural results. It is now our duty to record a still more marked, unlooked for, and astonishing manifestation of the effects of overpowering conviction which was witnessed on the morning of

Tuesday, in one of the departments of a most extensive spinning and manufacturing concern, which employs a vast number of workers, male and female.

"The young women engaged in the department we referred to are not mill workers and are generally of a respectable class. Some of them are Sabbath scholars and these, among others, had attended revival meetings. Within two or three hours on the morning mentioned nearly twenty of these girls were struck down, each in an instant at their work; several becoming apparently insensible at once and others uttering agonising cries for mercy. The scene produced the greatest excitement throughout the entire works, and not a little alarm. The persons prostrated were, however, promptly attended to by the humane manager and by their companions. Cars were provided for those who could not otherwise be moved to their homes, and the rest were assisted out of the premises and taken to their respective places of abode.

"Orders were given that the work rooms should be closed for the day, and some additional cases of visitation occurred, even as the young women were leaving the place and passing down the stairs. Some of those convicted have not yet been able to return to work. In most cases on reaching home, the persons affected, or their friends, sought spiritual and some of them medical advice, and when prayer had been offered up in a majority of instances speedy relief both from physical and mental suffering appeared to be produced. Several of the young women, we have been informed, have found peace and a number are earnestly seeking it in prayer.

"We regret to hear that a most unpleasant occurrence took place in connection with the manifestation. It is stated that, as the gates stood open to allow the workers to pass out, a clergyman of high standing in town was passing and, observing one of his own hearers among those who had been stricken down, entered to make enquiries respecting her, when he was accosted by two of the proprietors and received a very curt and impolite statement that his services were not required – a statement which caused him instantly to leave. This incident has been the subject of general comment for the last few days.

"Several further cases of conviction and conversion have happened in Ewart's Mill and other manufacturers on the same road. It is with concern we have to state that very bold, if not actually illegal, measures have been taken in one of them, with whose sanction we know not. It appears that the workers were warned that if they dared to attend any revival meeting they immediately would be discharged. One little boy, we are told, was seen pointing out a passage of scripture to two female workers when the manager took the Bible from him, locked it up and, in the evening, discharged all three. If this be true, we have no doubt they will easily find employment and better treatment elsewhere.

"It has been reported to us that in a large mill on the Falls Road, where several cases of awakening have taken place, equally harsh and stringent steps have been resorted to, to frighten the workers from joining in the movement, or from daring to yield to a Power beyond their control. We have heard however that the order, having proved utterly useless, has been rescinded. Another incident with similar interference to work people has been talked of, which is said to have occurred in a weaving factory. We may mention that the managers in all of these concerns are stated to be Roman Catholics. A number of the other mills in town, where the work of revival has reached, a very different course of conduct has been pursued towards the workers."

Interesting Incidents

"During Tuesday night some remarkable cases came under the attention of the gentlemen engaged in the work of visitation. About ten o'clock on that night a visit was paid to the house of a respectable family residing in the neighbourhood of Peter's Hill. One of the female members of the family – a young woman of about eighteen years – was affected on Friday last and has since recovered from her illness. When the visitors entered she was still confined to bed, but received them with great warmth of feeling. She then requested that they would join with her in singing the 40th Psalm and in prayer. She made the prayer herself and her language was so solemn and affecting that in this small company of fifteen or sixteen people there was not a dry eye, many gave vent to their feelings in loud and earnest sobbings for their sins. She expressed all confidence in her Saviour and stated to those present that her position in the afterlife would bear testimony that she felt the greatness of His mercy.

"After she had concluded, her sister, who had not previously been under such influence, requested those present to remain while she prayed and this also was full of the most spiritual sentiment and truth. Before the visitors left, the young woman, who was in a state of illness, requested all present who had not found the Saviour to seek Him earnestly and they would find Him, for He was a loving Saviour. 'Oh!' she said, 'If you had received one of His embraces, as I have received them, you would not only love Him through this short period of your lives, but throughout eternity.' She was then, with this prayerful proceeding, somewhat exhausted and the visitors left with the impression upon their minds that this was a striking example of the glorious fruits of the movement.

"About eleven o'clock on Tuesday night the same gentlemen entered Leeds Street. There they found groups of people anxiously awaiting the arrival of ministers or elders, who could afford consolation and comfort to those who had been stricken down. In one of the houses, into which they entered, they found a strong, powerful man who had made a visit for the purpose of conducting prayer, struck down and crying for mercy. Those present stated that, while in the midst of his prayer, he fell down into the state in which he was then found. While prayer was being conducted in this house, the visitors were called upon to attend another person in the same street who was also suffering from a like influence. The latter person was left in a state of mental agony.

"In the neighbourhood of Sandy Row there were three remarkable cases on Tuesday – one was of a Roman Catholic, another was a Presbyterian and the third was a member of the Established Church. At two o'clock yesterday morning all that could possibly be done to bring peace and joy to the minds of these people had been effected.

"The movement is not confined to the humble dwellings of mill workers and others of the lower industrial classes. A case has come to our knowledge in which a lady of independent means has felt the power of the awakening Spirit and yielded to His influence. In another incident four female servants, in a first class hotel, have been deeply and almost simultaneously impressed and are now in a hopeful frame of mind, after having been visited and prayed for by a minister and elder.

"A working man, residing in a street off the Shankill Road, received a powerful impression and was in deep distress of mind. Some mischievous person sent to the house a fiddler, who commenced to play. This wanton and cruel joke threw the poor man into despair. He was afterwards visited by a clergyman, under whose consolation he soon recovered and found peace.

"An old man, once a publican who had long neglected worship, latterly attended it, became convicted after having been deeply affected, and now rejoices in the knowledge of his Saviour. A young man aged twenty one, who had been a Sabbath-breaker, and a drunkard, was visited by the Spirit on Saturday, and on Sunday he was found addressing a meeting. Immediately upon finding peace, he exclaimed:– 'My wild career is over forever.' Some of his wicked companions visited him and, after he had told them what God had done for him, he encouraged them to join him in singing a Psalm. Some of them have since been attending the meetings.

"Another who has confessed himself to have been a 'white-washed hypocrite,' was visited by God at the family altar. God is now precious to his soul and is unceasing in visitation.

"A man, the father of a family, was convicted, then found peace and is now visiting others; his wife has also become convicted of sin through the prayers of a devout Christian.

"A young widow in easy circumstances and a girl who was known to her had both been converted and, overtaking one another on the Falls Road, rushed into each other's arms, before a number of passers-by burst into tears and offered their mutual Christian congratulations.

"Another instance of Christian love was exhibited by a young man who, on meeting an exhorter, grasped his hand warmly and told him of what God had done for himself, his mother and sister.

"A Roman Catholic man, working in a mill, was prostrated at his employment and carried home. This is believed to be a genuine case of conviction. A Roman Catholic girl was similarly affected, and is now thoroughly converted. Her exclamation is:– 'No Virgin for me!'"

Revivals and Cock-Fighting

"On Tuesday the 7th there was a glorious meeting at Creaghrock – midway between Ahoghill and Randalstown. This place has become famous, or rather infamous, as a cock pit especially on Ahoghill Old Fair Day, when thousands would have assembled for the degrading sport of cock-fighting, thereby making it a scene of lying, blasphemy, drunkenness and all manner of sin. In these revival times a number of the awakened, some of whom perhaps were 'cockers' themselves, resolved to make on this occasion a far different scene, and therefore invited several ministers to attend and address the meeting against all manner of vice, and further promotion of all manner of holiness. Tuesday was one of June's finest days – sky unclouded, sun brilliant, all nature laughing with joy, and 'Heaven smiling o'er us.'

"The meeting was at ten o'clock in the morning and even at that early hour crowds in all directions and of all characters – in many cases from a distance of five or six miles – were seen wending their way gladly to the rock, and at one time there could not have been much less than two thousand present. All behaved with good manners, while the Rev. Mr. Smith of Creaghmore, the Rev. Messrs. D. Adams and F. Buick of Ahoghill and the Rev. H. Stewart usefully and earnestly addressed the vast and attentive audience, while prayers were offered up by fervent laymen. A most solemn impression was produced on all from the grey-haired man of ninety to the merry child of a few years. Many of the old and young were deeply and visibly impressed by the Spirit's power and, altogether, such hallowed scenes cannot fail to be engraved on the heart of every participant, as it is believed that several on that day could then and there look up to Heaven and say of Jesus, 'Rock of Ages, Cleft for me.'"

"The Banner of Ulster" Saturday, 11th June 1859

"We are obliged to present such a summary of the most important and useful information on the subject of the revivals at large, as our judgement enables us to select from the mass of details we have ourselves gleaned or which have been furnished by others.

"Those of 'little faith' in the astonishing movement which is now going forward will not, we presume, hesitate to give credence to the irrefutable evidence of statistics in its favour. An item of such evidence we shall present. The temperance cause has gained much observance during the few weeks that have elapsed since the commencement of the revivals, than it did in as many months previously. A number of public houses, which opened their floodgates of vice and immorality during the permitted hours of the Sabbath, now keep their doors closed all Sabbath long, for lack of customers. The number of cases of drunkenness brought under the notice of the magistrates from day to day are, consequently, decreasing – a proof of which we hope those gentlemen will not lose sight in their observations from the bench, that wherever the revivals have originated or may spread, there is something in them after all, which is not to be lightly spoken of."

"The Ballymena Observer" Saturday, 11th June 1859

"We paid a short visit to the Presbyterian Church in Wellington Street at a very late hour one evening this week, and a description of what we observed, on that occasion, would be similar to the proceedings of almost every other evening for the last fortnight. We passed toward the church but found entrance was impossible, for the pews in every portion of the church were crowded to excess, the aisles completely filled, and the vestibule occupied with anxious listeners. The number present could not have been less than two thousand.

"Passing toward the rear of the church we found a throng of people assembled about every window, and, having succeeded in obtaining admission to the vestry room, we there beheld a scene which it would be impossible to forget, but equally impossible to describe. The apartment was literally filled, with people of both sexes who had been borne from the church under the most excruciating agonies of strong conviction – some of them in a fainting state – some prostrate and moaning heavily – some calling upon the Name of the Lord Jesus – some praying for grace and faith – and others crying aloud in a frenzied supplication for Heaven's mercy. In one corner of the room we observed a grey-haired old man, trembling in every limb and regardless of all around him, fervently and audibly imploring God to pardon his manifold transgressions, for the Redeemer's sake. A boy, some fourteen or fifteen years of age, was reeling in fearful agony of mind upon the floor calling persistently for mercy and for deliverance from the expected torments of an anticipated Hell. 'Oh, Saviour of sinners,' he exclaimed, 'deliver me from this horrible pit!' 'Oh, Jesus of Nazareth, set my feet upon that rock!' In another part of the room a young man, in low and solemn tones, gave expression to his feeling in the following language:- 'I know that my Redeemer liveth – I know that He can save my soul – I know that He can wash me from all uncleanness in the fountain of His atoning blood; but oh, I have crucified Him – I have crucified Him! I have despised His holy Name, and how shall I approach Him! Oh, my sins, my sins! Oh God, be merciful to me a sinner!'

"A solemn influence had fallen upon every heart. Many people, unused to such an attitude at public worship, were humbly kneeling in pews, aisles, and window recesses of the gallery on which we stood, and we observed that a decently retired female had prostrated herself full length upon the pulpit stairs. In the course of this prayer a case of sudden conviction occurred in close proximity to the very spot we occupied. The person was an aged woman, who gave loud expression to her sensations in mournful cries, beseeching the Lord Jesus to have mercy upon her sinful soul. She bowed her face upon her quivering hands and we could perceive that scalding tears were trickling through her withered fingers. All the while, 'Oh, Saviour, pity me' was the burden of her prayer. The church was not vacated until past midnight."

"The Ballymena Observer" Saturday, 18th June 1859

"Among the many good results of this general awakening, we may remark that the ordinary Sabbath-day services of public worship are attended by crowds of people once regardless of everything, except their wellbeing at that time, but now deeply anxious respecting their future position in eternity. At the Presbyterian Church in Wellington Street the congregation was so numerous, in the forenoon of Sunday last, that many people were unable to obtain admission – and four or five new cases of 'convictions' occurred during the celebration of public worship.

"In the evening an immense crowd of the community assembled for united prayer, in a grass park to the west of Galgorm Road, a locality very suitable to the people. All the churches in Ballymena would not have contained the number present, and the spectacle was one of the most solemn and interesting that we have ever witnessed. From the position occupied by the speakers, the velvet-like meadow sloped gently upward in the form of a semi-circle amphitheatre, and the audience comprising of all classes and denominations of people, occupied the premises in line over line, presenting a vast audience of human beings too numerous for calculation. It was a scene well intended to make a serious impression upon every heart, and an abiding one upon the memory, so we are totally unable to describe it.

"The entire crowd appeared to be under the solemn influence of the devotional Spirit, but without any extravagance of speech or gesture. At first view, they appeared as if rooted to the ground on which they stood. There was no motion perceptible among the mass – no whispering among the awe stricken multitude – no romping of children about the outskirts; for the proclamation of the gospel message appeared to have arrested the attention of all present, and the greater number of them had Bibles.

"The services were opened by the Rev. S. J. Moore, after which addresses followed in succession from four or five lay converts. Their language was characterised by the unpolished but effective eloquence of nature – but they were thoroughly in earnest. We understand that several strong marked cases of sudden conviction occurred while these exhortations were in progress. But the parties so affected had been carried to a remote corner of the field. The services were brought to a conclusion by the Rev. Moore, who called upon the audience to unite in the singing of an appropriate hymn, and forthwith the response of voices of the assembled multitude rose high in a solemn swell – in heart touching appeals of praise to the Omnipotent.

"Prayer and benediction followed, but the audience did not separate, for strange and most exciting scenes immediately ensued. Suddenly one person, and then another, and another, in rapid succession, fell to the ground with piercing cries of agony. It soon spread further among the crowd, and within half an hour we found that not fewer than twenty human beings exhibited emotions, both of soul and body, sufficient to dismay the stoutest heart. Remorse for sin – an overwhelming sense of the impending danger – a frightful conviction that they were on the downward road to everlasting destruction – and that no power, except that of God in Christ could bring help or salvation – was the overriding 'impression' upon them all.

"Then followed loud impulsive cries for the Redeemer's mercy expressed in tones of anguish, which no imagination can induce or pen describe – to comprehend the depth of their intensity those cries must be heard and once heard they can never be forgotten.

"We may remark that three days afterwards a woman was visited by a Christian friend, who had been the witness of her agony. He found her weak in body, but her mind was thoroughly composed. She was a new creature. The light of peace and love was beaming from her face, and joy flashed in her eyes as she told him of her perfect reconciliation with God, and her unwavering faith in the Redeemer. She expressed her consciousness that the power of the Holy Spirit had been exercised upon her heart, and she blessed God that He had brought her to repentance, and salvation (in His Own way). She had seen the exceeding sinfulness of sin.

"Minor differences among the evangelical clergy appear to have been entirely forgotten in their common desire for the conversion of souls and the extension of Christ's Kingdom. This union, upon their part, is hailed with great satisfaction by every denomination of the Protestant laity.

"The converts from Roman Catholicism continue in steady adherence to the reformed doctrines wherewith they have been impressed and it is a significant fact that one of them, very recently, took a leading part in a public prayer meeting near Broughshane. Many seriously minded members of the Roman Catholic Church attend the revival meetings in Ballymena and the neighbourhood – but they do so in defiance of certain stern injunctions to the contrary. We know of one poor boy who was inhumanly beaten by his parents for disregarding this ban. When thus compelled to obedience he, although unable to read, purchased a copy of the New Testament Scriptures, and presented it to a godly old neighbour still poorer than himself, on whom he attends to hear a portion of it read at every available opportunity."

Origin of the Revival

"A correspondent residing at Castlegore, Connor, sent us the following interesting particulars:– 'In the immediate neighbourhood of Kells is a schoolhouse where, assembled every Friday evening during the Autumn of 1857, four men, who are comparatively young, held a 'believer's fellowship meeting' – their special object being prayer to God that He would bless their labours in connection with the prayer meetings, and Sabbath Schools, which they had organised. For some time there appeared no answer to their prayers but, like the Patriarch of old, they were determined to wrestle with the Almighty until He would bless them. At length God, Who is ever the hearer and answerer of the supplications of His people, graciously assured them that the fruits of their labours would be seen springing up around them.

"'About the beginning of January 1858 a youth, who had attended a class in a Sabbath School taught by J.M. (who was one of the first affected by this movement, and is now employed as a missionary among the people) was the first who was brought to the saving knowledge of the grace of God. Others were converted, one by one, until they were numbered by tens. The movement became so successful that, in a short time, it numbered its hundreds, now thousands and, in all human probability, tens of thousands will be the result of that small beginning, this verifying the prophecy 'a little one shall become a thousand'.

"'Having spread so wonderfully about Kells, and Connor, and the surrounding country, in other places the people began to enquire after the marvellous workings of God there. Many, from distances, came and amongst these was one man named S.C. who sought very anxiously for the salvation of his soul, and prayed earnestly for it. God heard and answered his prayers. Like the woman at the well with her Lord, he was determined to tell others to 'come and see' that Saviour Who had done so much for his soul. At first he traced his steps towards home so that he could tell his family, consisting of a widow mother, brothers, and sisters, of what the Lord had done for him. His warnings to them were not in vain for God blessed his effort, and made him the instrument in His Hand of turning them from sin, and unto holiness. He did not rest satisfied with the good work, which he had been the means of commencing at home, but he told his neighbours around of a loving Saviour able and willing to redeem them, if they would but look to Him for salvation.

"'It was thus that revival spread to Ahoghill, and I have been told categorically that, for miles around, multitudes of anxious souls are seeking salvation. The Roman Catholics, who have been brought under conviction, are embracing as their Mediator the Lord and Saviour Jesus Christ, and denouncing popery and all its errors. Many instances of this class might be quoted but one will suffice. A young man who had been converted and who has faithfully, like a true soldier of the Cross, withstood all the temptations that had been brought to bear upon him from friends, and also from the energetic endeavours of the Priests to bring him back to the fold of the Roman Catholic Church addressed a large audience last Sabbath evening in the townland Tanaybrake. It may be stated that the Priests are doing their very utmost to prevent their people from attending any of the services conducted by the converts.'"

A Spread of Religious Awakenings in Killymorris

"We have received the following letter from Rev. John Wilson of Killymorris:-

"'It affords me much pleasure being able to inform you, the religious awakening has made rapid progress and been most beneficial in its results. Having opened a class for the instruction and comfort of recent converts, I was much gratified to find both old and young freely enter it. Never have I met a more interesting class – one of such anxious enquirers and apparently so deeply impressed with divine truth. The keen desire manifested for the reading of the Bible, and the Scriptural views expressed by the converted, give strong evidence that the work is from Him Who has said, 'Search the Scriptures; for in them ye think ye have eternal life: and they are they which testify of Me.' Visiting a family, in which were three children who had passed through the ordeal of deep conviction, the father said to me 'he had just been reading to his children an account of the revival as given in the memoir of McCheyne, but he saw their attention was lost and could only be regained by reading to them from the Bible.

"'Going down the other evening to Portrush, I found in the train many with Bibles in their hands and heard them sing some of the sweet songs of Zion.

"'Our weekly congregational prayer meetings, and all the prayer meetings about here, are largely attended. I went to the townland of ___ to establish a weekly prayer meeting, where formerly there had been none. We met a large congregation, so many assembled, we were under the necessity of holding the meeting in the open-air, and such was the desire of the people for prayer that instead of one prayer meeting we needed two, for they said, 'No house could hold us.' These meetings are generally conducted by experienced leaders. Reading the scriptures, prayer, and praise are the principal worship. A young man said to us that Christ came to him as he lay alone in an open field, bathed in tears on account of his sins, and spoke peace to his troubled soul, and that he would not exchange the peace he now had for the brightest of earthly thrones. He also added that he had experienced more pleasure and delight in the House of God for the past two Sabbaths than almost all his time before. Finding the reason, he came to worship God, Who is Spirit, in Spirit and in truth.'"

"The Coleraine Chronicle" Saturday, 18th June 1859

Ballyrashane

"The Rev. John Alexander has kindly furnished us with the following note on the progress of the revival in his own neighbourhood:– 'Since Monday night this district has been in the greatest state of excitement. In different localities prayer meetings have been held and numerously attended. The first meeting was held at Damhead, when several persons came under the influence of this extraordinary dispensation. In the Parish of Ballyrashane, on the leading road down to Portrush, nearly every family has been visited. In some cases only one member and in other incidents the whole family has been brought under conviction. I have seen cholera, and afterwards famine rage in frightful forms around us, but never did I see a tenth part of the excitement which I have witnessed for the last ten days. The last Sabbath at Ballyrashane, the service in the meeting house was one not to be forgotten by any who were present. There was a crowd of anxious and deeply impressed hearers. A few people came under the influence of conviction which occasioned a little confusion, but the effect was most extraordinary. I had previously announced an outdoor sermon for last Sabbath evening at Ballybogey, and it was afterwards made known that the meeting would be attended and addressed by some of the 'awakened'. I arrived at the place at the appointed hour, and such a multitude I have seldom witnessed. There were, it was considered, fifteen hundred people on the ground. Excellent addresses were delivered by Messrs. MacAfee and Boyle, and others. Upwards of fifty people were convicted at the meeting. The scene, apart from its moral results, was truly alarming.

"Prayer meetings have been held every evening this week at Cloyfinn, Ballyrashane Meeting House and Damhead. The moral effect in this district is beyond all description. The ministers have been employed in leading and guiding meetings – this they have done harmoniously, prayerfully and practically, both day and night. The cases are numerous and important. Comment here is useless, and all around are equally well acquainted with this extraordinary and merciful dispensation. It is a great good work of the Spirit of God, and I firmly believe that great and good will be the results.'"

Coleraine

"The new town hall – the manner of celebrating the completion of which had, a few weeks ago, given no little anxiety to our more public-spirited townsmen – was opened in a most unexpected and still more gratifying way than could have been anticipated. Instead of the joyous dance and the stirring and enlivening music of the ballroom, which, with all its glitter, could not have satisfied the heart of any of those who might in the enjoyment of the hour have delighted – the walls of the hall gave back the almost despairing groan of a stricken sinner, the heart-felt prayer of a believing repentant – all resounded with the adoring thanks of a redeemed saint.

"Continual watching and labour had, towards an advanced hour of the morning, thinned the room of the band of comforters which, up 'til then, had been untiring in their attempts at consolation. But to us who visited it at intervals during the night, from midnight, the scene was indescribable. A melancholic beauty attached to it which was saddening and beautiful in the extreme – saddening because in more than one incident we saw a struggling soul battling for the victory over sin without a solitary individual to speak comfort – and beautiful because we felt confidence in the result, believing that God 'Who tempers the wind in the shorn lamb' would, in His Own good time, bring relief through the peace-speaking blood of the atonement.

"Nightly vigils, which had wearied ministers and others, could not quench the love of a mother – for six long hours we saw in the niche of a window a mother sitting with her afflicted son's head in her lap waiting until God Who had long been with him, 'waiting to be gracious,' should think it right to give him a sight of the Cross. A view of the sacrifice on Calvary was, at last, vouched safe, and the young man who had been guilty of many offences – many open violations of God's Law – awoke to consciousness believing in the great atonement and rejoicing that even such a sinner as he could be received by the Lamb of God. We have seen him many times since and we have no hesitation in saying that a life-long reformation has been wrought in him, because we heard him with joy in his countenance, declaring that things which formerly gave him pleasure, he could no longer delight in."

"The Belfast Newsletter" Monday morning, 20th June 1859

A Field Meeting

"At three o'clock yesterday afternoon a field meeting was held, in the field opposite Eglinton Street and adjoining Old Lodge Road. Although rain was falling at the time, yet about three thousand people attended and remained during the service, while several hundreds left, owing to the unfavourable state of the weather; and it is not too much to suppose that, had the day been fine, it would have been the largest religious meeting which has ever been assembled in Belfast. The religious worship was conducted by the Rev. William Arthur. Singing and prayer formed the chief portion of the proceedings, as it was considered best to terminate the meeting speedily, as the evening was wet. The Rev. Robert Wallace delivered a very short address and, then concluding, called upon those present, who wished to show that they were for Christ, to kneel down during the prayer, and this appeal was responded to by the vast congregation – formed of all ranks, classes, and ages – kneeling down *en masse* on the ground, while the Rev. Mr. Bollard offered up a most earnest prayer. The scene was one of the most solemn and impressive character, not to be easily forgotten by those who were present."

Open-air Preaching

"Saturday last an open-air service was conducted in Sandy Row by the Rev. W. C. Campbell and other Wesleyan ministers, when a very touching sermon was preached from Ezekiel 32:11. During the delivery of the sermon many became deeply moved and, at the close, several went forward to chairs which had been set for those who were convicted to kneel at and, of these, four professed to have experienced pardon before leaving. Yesterday, at four o'clock the Rev. John White preached in the sheds opposite the Custom House to a very large congregation and many, during the delivery of the sermon, were moved to tears. Open-air services were also held in other parts of the town and, in all of these, large congregations assembled."

"The Banner of Ulster" Tuesday, 21st June 1859

Belfast

"The revival services are now almost common in the evangelical churches throughout the city and are held nearly every weekday evening and several times on the Sabbath, and prayer meetings take place in many quarters in private houses. All these are attended by crowds of deeply anxious audiences, who return time after time and carry home impressions which ripen into yearnings after those things that are profitable for salvation. Empty or partially filled pews are now as rare on Sundays, in some houses of worship, as were fully occupied ones not many weeks ago. It is a most pleasing sight to witness the throngs who, every Sabbath, crowd the thoroughfares on their way to the House of God, compared with the numbers who were formerly attracted by 'the sound of the church going bell'.

"The practice long, as common as it was reprehensible, of persons spending one portion of the Lord's Day in religious worship and the rest on unprofitable recreation has greatly abated and given way to the reading of the scriptures and home prayer. Heads of families, who were formerly careless as to the manner in which their children spent the Sabbath or as to how it was employed by themselves, are now to be found leading the youthful train to church and raising the voice in praise and prayer at the domestic altar. These must be God's doings and, as such, they are truly marvellous in the eyes of all who regard them aright.

"Some persons who look upon the revivals but to ridicule and misrepresent them, have put in circulation the more absurd and unfounded reports respecting them. Most of these are not worth our while to notice or expose, but one of them is so grossly groundless and mischievous in nature that it is our duty to contradict it. A statement has been put forward from a group, from which more candour was to have been anticipated, to the effect that some of the people who had been prostrated had become deranged and are now inmates in the lunatic asylum. We have authority for stating that there is not one word of truth in this report.

"It is highly gratifying to know that the Episcopalian clergy in the city are entering fully into the movement, and exerting themselves actively to promote it. The work will be seen, from the communications we send, to be spreading rapidly in various districts of the country and with the most blessed effects. It is attracting serious attention on the other side of the channel."

Lisburn

"A correspondent states:- 'The wonderful spread of renewed vitality in sacred things has, at length, reached Lisburn; and, though no great manifestations have yet been exhibited, there are ample evidences that the good work has commenced. On Sabbath last the Presbyterian Church was crowded to excess and the new church (Episcopalian) was so thronged that numbers had to go away for want of room. The Cathedral was also very largely attended, and the congregations at the different sections of the Wesleyans were much above their ordinary numbers.

"At about three o'clock in the afternoon a public meeting was held in a large field immediately adjoining the spinning mill of Messrs. R. Stewart & Sons. At this meeting an immense crowd attended. After an introductory address by Mr. R. Stewart one of those individuals who had lately been aroused into active life in ministerial affairs stood up and delivered a very remarkable discourse to the assembled multitude. His sermon was plain and practical without anything exciting in its language, but there was an earnestness of feeling, in the form of delivery, which spoke effectively to all within sound of the preacher's voice. Four people were suddenly arrested in the unusual manner, calling aloud for the grace of the Spirit and the mercy of

God. Many others gave evidence of the great work which has begun in the town of Lisburn.

"The evening services in all the Protestant places of worship were attended by increased numbers, all seemingly anxious to hear the Word of truth, and over the face of each congregation was a degree of seriousness such as has hardly ever before been seen in this place. In the meantime all the ministers are up and doing. The Dean of Ross and curates have taken up the subject in right earnestness. The Rev. Mr. Breakey, who has carefully guarded against all attempts to create any undue excitement, will hold a meeting in his church on Friday next, on which occasion two of the young men from the neighbourhood of Ballymena are expected to address the people on the present remarkable stirring up of Christian worship in all the churches. The Methodist congregations have also purposed to have special services during the week."

Islandmagee

"In Islandmagee the revival movement has made great progress. The first manifestation was on Wednesday, 8ᵗʰ June, the day of humiliation prior to the Lord's Supper in the church of the 1ˢᵗ congregation. Many came up to the House of God that day – they could not tell how it was – with a more than ordinary feeling of holy reverence and anxious expectation. The Rev. George McGill of Lylehill officiated. The services were not long commenced when a young lady was smitten down. From that day, to the present hour, God has been walking throughout the length and width of the district, subduing stubborn hearts, and awakening many who were at ease in Zion.

"The 1ˢᵗ and 2ⁿᵈ Presbyterian Churches are now filled to overflowing. The Lord's Supper was held in the church of the 1ˢᵗ congregation on the second Sabbath of this month and such a solemn communion the members of the congregation never experienced on any former occasion. On the Monday evening following there was a prayer meeting. Hundreds attended and many were convicted. On Wednesday evening another meeting was held at Rev. Mr. Campbell's church. About nine hundred were present. The meeting was addressed by the Rev. Messrs. Campbell, Whiteford, Warwick, and Shaw. Many were awakened and many were stricken down. Hundreds remained about the House of God 'til the sun had risen. On Thursday evening the 2nd Presbyterian Church was filled to overflowing. The Rev. Mr. R. H. Shaw presided. The meeting was addressed by the Rev. Mr. W. Campbell, David Andrews, and others. The feeling was intense. On Sabbath last the Lord's Supper was administered in Mr. Shaw's church. The attendance was large. In both the 1st and 2nd congregations the number there sharing in the Lord's Supper was greatly increased. During the last twelve days in the district many have been savingly brought to God and many more, who are yet in doubt and darkness, we trust shall before long, know Christ as a personal Saviour. Prayer meetings are being established in localities all over the district."

Limavady

"In Limavady and its surrounding district the deep feeling on the subject of religion, which has been appearing in other places, has manifested itself with great intensity. The first cases of deep anxiety of mind, manifested visibly by the bodily weakness and agony which arrest the thoughtless, occurred in Limavady on the 8th. At meetings on the 10th and 11th there were still more. On Sabbath the 12th and subsequently in Limavady, Ballykelly, Largy, Bovevagh, Myroe the feelings of religious anxiety have been intense. Prayer meetings are held every night and such is the feeling of the people that, generally, they will not break up 'til after midnight. At these meetings sometimes as many as forty or fifty have fallen down, some screaming for mercy and others remaining for hours in speechless agony.

"Even in rural districts there is the same desire to meet and wait on God, and the same remarkable manifestations. Those who had been thus suddenly arrested and brought under strong convictions of the horrors of sin, to Christ, speak afterwards of their great joy, and great earnestness in inviting others to come to Jesus and in praying for them. Their simple addresses seemed to be particularly acknowledged. Their desire to tell what God has done for their souls seemed almost irrepressible. The language used by one young man will give an idea of the feeling of all. Speaking of the change that had passed on him he said, 'At the beginning of the week, if my minister had told me that I was on the road to Hell, I would have been so angry that I would have left his church. Now I would rejoice to stand up in the public congregation and tell them what a sinner I was, and what a Saviour I have found.'

"Some of the worst characters in the place had been convicted of sin and brought, as it were, to the Saviour. The sensation produced was great, beyond description; preacher and people both seemed, for the time, overpowered by a sense of the peculiar presence of God. The meeting was addressed by the minister of the Presbyterian Church in Ballyclare by one of the new converts, by a friend from Belfast (an elder in Rev. Mr. Toye's congregation), and by the Methodist minister of the town, by whom the outdoor services of the evening were concluded. During the time of service, the friends and spectators, who crowded into the church to assist or observe those who were labouring under the terrible influences of conviction, so filled the building that it became heated almost to suffocation, and to avoid the consequences naturally resulting from such an atmosphere – consequences which had begun to appear, as several fainted where they stood – it became absolutely necessary not only to refuse admittance to those who were anxious to enter, but also to request all who were merely spectators within to withdraw.

"After some struggling and wrestling with God in prayer, many, we have reason to know, found peace and joy in believing and returned to their homes rejoicing; but not 'til the late hour of midnight did the voice of praise and prayer cease to be heard within the House of God and far on into the morning; and from houses, where such sounds never issued before, might be heard the singing of Psalms and hymns, falling upon the ear with a heart-softening power, as it broke the solemn stillness that reigned around. Wonderful, indeed, is the change that has been produced upon this town – so wonderful, that even the ungodly and indifferent have been constrained to say, 'The Hand of the Lord has wrought this."

"The Banner of Ulster" Thursday, 23rd June 1859

Newtownards

"We are happy to state that the expectation of a revival in this town is being now finally fulfilled. Symptoms of a revival had been, for some time previously, displayed but it was not until last week that any very decided manifestation of Divine Power appeared. The weekly meeting for united prayer was held in the Rev. Mr. McCullough's church, and the intense interest excited was shown by the fact that it was one of the largest that ever assembled in this spacious building. This interest was deepened by the news that arrived daily from Comber of the outpouring of the Spirit on members of the Rev. Mr. Killen's church, and particularly by a case of a woman belonging to that place who had been attending the meetings held there on Friday evening and had come over to Newtownards on Saturday morning when she was suddenly prostrated in the Market Square.

"Since that time there have been a very considerable number of cases of conviction, followed, in most of the incidents, by conversion. Prayer meetings are being daily held in almost all the churches and several private houses in different districts of the town. The incidents of the revival are even already numerous and striking. People who have doubted its reality have become, at once, convinced of its genuine character, when they saw and conversed with people who had been affected – in this way the statement is frequently verified that, 'seeing is believing'. The change which passes over the character of those who had been truly awakened is marvellous.

"A visitor was astonished, on entering a house, of a person he had known as one of those who are without God in the world, to find him with the Bible in his hand, strengthening his own faith in the reality of his conversion by pointing to examples, from scripture, of salvation obtained by the chief of sinners. He was also surprised to meet with individuals whose hearts have been changed, who had not been, for a long time, in the habit of attending any place of worship. They had heard of the Spirit's work in other places and, without any Philip to guide them, they had taken down the dusty Bible from the shelf and found it to be able to make them wise unto salvation.

"Nothing indeed connected with the movement is more remarkable than the Sovereignty of the Spirit. He chooses whom He will, and works in them how He will. The outwardly moral and openingly profane, the old and the young seem to be all equally capable, if He pleases, of becoming the subjects of Divine grace. One of the happiest incidents indeed of the revival here is the case of a little child, scarcely more than ten years of age. The child was being questioned, by a minister, on the meaning of the opening address of the 'Lord's Prayer', and in order to illustrate the love due to our Father in Heaven by the love rendered to an earthly parent, he asked her, 'Is your father loving?' 'Yes.' 'Do you love your father?' 'Of course I do.' 'There is no one I suppose whom you love better than your father?' 'Yes. I love Christ more' was the unexpected reply. 'I love Christ more' is a matter of thankfulness that the movement has been, so far, largely characterised by the absence of any great physical prostration."

"The Derry Sentinel" Friday, 24th June 1859

Dungiven

"A revival meeting was held on the 17th in the Presbyterian Meeting House, Dungiven, which had to be adjourned to a field on accord of the numbers there being upwards of one thousand people. The devotional worship was conducted by the Rev. Messrs. McGill, Black and Davison, and the local Presbyterian clergymen were ably assisted by several laymen. The manifestations on the occasion were truly astounding. Not less than one hundred persons were convicted, and were able to cry for mercy. I am happy to state that one Roman Catholic bewailed his lost condition and fled to the Cross of Christ for refuge. I consider about three quarters, or more, of those stricken, rejoiced in a Saviour's love before they left the place, which was about four o'clock next morning.

"There was also a prayer meeting held by the Rev. George Scott of Banagher on Monday, 20th at Banagher, at which there were some eight persons converted. We had also a meeting in the Parish Church of Dungiven on the 22nd, attended by some four or five hundred people – all of whom appeared to be deeply affected by a most eloquent, impressive and heart touching sermon delivered by the Rev. George Scott, who preached from Revelation 3:20. Altogether the inhabitants of this locality, even those not convicted, appeared to be living more consistent lives, and God has manifested Himself in our midst breaking the most stubborn and hard sinner's heart."

"The Banner of Ulster" Saturday, 25th June 1859

Limavady

"A great number of Roman Catholics have been converted in and around this town. A great sensation was created here amongst the Romanists on learning that three young ladies, daughters of a gentleman who holds a government position in the town, had been struck down and, through the grace of God, were converted to Christ – and, of course, refused to enter any place of worship where the creature was worshipped instead of the Creator. In spite of all threats they have refused to kneel to any, but the One true God. On Friday last, seven people in the workhouse were struck down, four of whom were Romanists but the Priest strove to persuade them that it was merely weakness, but in vain; they still cried for the great High Priest, who alone can bring comfort to the wounded heart. They have all, thank God, been plucked as brands from the burning. The Priests here have used all the means in their power to prevent any other people attending our open-air meetings; but, thank God, a spirit of enquiry has entered the minds of the people and they will not be prevented from attending, where knowledge can be obtained."

"The Ballymena Observer" Saturday, 25th June 1859

"On the evening of Sunday last another open-air meeting for prayer and exhortation was held at Ballymena. The ground was moist and slight rain showers were falling at intervals, nevertheless three thousand people of Ballymena, and adjoining districts, were assembled at seven o'clock. Some young converts addressed the audience in a very earnest manner chiefly in reference to their own former habits of life 'without God in the world' and the wonderful evidence of a mighty power as displayed in the circumstances of their own conversion. They explained fully that the only means of salvation as provided is the full, perfect and sufficient atonement of the Lord Jesus Christ and described in glowing and spontaneous language the unspeakable happiness arising from a heart-felt consciousness of peace with God and fellowship with the Redeemer.

"Shortly after nine o'clock the regular service of the evening was brought to a conclusion, but the greater part of the audience did not separate until nearly eleven o'clock as a result of what ensued. Six or eight individuals, among the audience, were suddenly prostrated, uttering cries of agonising remorse and loudly beseeching God, for Christ's sake, to pardon their iniquities.

"One poor girl was praying fervently, and her hands were clasped and elevated, her eyes were fixed upward, and the tone of her solemn voice was natural. Some of her expressions were to the following effect – 'Lord Jesus, I am a sinner, but Thou can save me!' 'Oh, pluck me as a brand from the burning!' 'I can do nothing – oh, I can do nothing for myself – but Thou art my Shield and my Redeemer – Thou art the Strong Rock of my salvation – oh, come to my relief – oh, come, come, come!'

"We heard another female voice exclaiming in tones of heart-rending despair – 'Oh, I am lost! I am lost!' 'I am a God-forsaken sinner!' 'Hell is wide open for me!' 'My wickedness is too great for pardon!' 'I cannot pray – oh, I have never prayed! I am lost – I am lost!' We could observe that a grey-haired man, apparently a minister of the gospel, was kneeling in silent prayer beside this conscious stricken woman, and then public prayer on her behalf was offered up by several godly laymen of the surrounding crowd.

"A young man, in a low and solemn tone of voice, gave expression to his feelings in the following language:– 'I know that my Redeemer liveth – I know that He can save my soul – I know that He can wash me from all uncleanness in the fountain of His atoning blood; but oh, I have crucified Him, I have crucified Him! I have despised His holy Name and how shall I approach Him! Oh, my sins, my sins! Oh God, be merciful to me, a sinner!'"

"The Belfast Newsletter" 25th June 1859

Revivals in Ulster

"The Rev. F. R. Trench, Rector of Newtown, Kells, Co. Meath, has published the following additional facts as to the revival movement:–

"'I have been told of the striking conversion of a notoriously wicked publican, living a mile from B___, where I walked to see him. He had been, as I partly learned from his own lips, a drunkard, a cock fighter in his youth, a card player, a blasphemer, and a man of immoral character in other ways. Approaching his house, I observed the pleasing mark of plaster, discoloured where the publican's signboard ten feet long, and which, I afterwards saw lying in the dung yard behind his house, had lately been affixed. The manner of W. L.'s conversion, as stated to me by himself was as follows:- He had been at a meeting where four converts had been speaking. He felt nothing particular then, but prayed, when he came home, that the Spirit would enlighten him. The next morning, when at breakfast, his family being present, the knife and fork on which he had a piece of meat fell out of his hands, and he fell prostrate. It was an hour or more before he was able even to cry for mercy. He determined, at once, to give up drinking, but did not decide on giving up the sale of spirits.

"'However, three weeks afterwards he was struck down still more violently at Mr. M's meeting, and was carried out by the minister and doctor to his sister-in-law's. He did not lie down until three or four in the morning, but got home in the course of the day, and that very day took down the licence and has neither sold nor tasted a drop of whiskey ever since, and has no desire for it nor ever had since he was first struck.'"

"The Newsletter" Monday morning, 27th June 1859

Coleraine

"Several cases of conviction have occurred in town since our last report, and the healthy influence, which the revival evoked is bearing rich fruit in the continued reformation of the people.

"One young man, who has been very unstable in the form of religion, professed he was stricken down in a wonderful manner on Saturday evening last. He was originally, by profession, a Protestant but, for the last five years, has proved himself a zealous member of the Roman Catholic Church. On Saturday night last, in company with another man, he had indulged to such an extent that he was not able to walk without assistance and, while in that state, he was heard to scoff at the manifestations of God's work amongst us, and to blaspheme at those who professed to have peace.

"We saw him whilst staggering under the influence of drink, and heard him revile his own mother because she would not provide him with some money to get drunk. He would not go into his own house, and we saw him assisted into that of a neighbour, where he slept for about one hour and a half when he got up for the purpose of extracting from his widowed mother 'another shilling'. While curses trembled on his lips, and the awakened thirst for strong drink drove him to disregard natural affection, the Hand of God was upon him and, before he reached the door, he was struck down in that mysterious way, uttering loud cries for mercy and pardon.

"Those around him, at first, ascribed to the delirium of drink the change in his appearance and talk, and did not, at first, take heed to what he said but when they heard him, with all the earnestness of his being, call upon God in prayer and saw that he had all at once by some mysterious power become perfectly sober, they at once 'took knowledge of him,' that the Spirit of God was at work in his soul. The people of the house then went in search of some good man to pray with him and when one did come and direct the stricken soul to the Lamb of God, through His Own Word, the transition in the house was wonderful – what a few minutes before was a drunken scene was now a house of prayer.

"Many who had known the youth, then suffering such agony of soul, gathered in and marvelled much at what they saw. The morning of the Sabbath dawned on a broken and contrite spirit and, when in the course of the day anxious friends and enquirers sought him in his own house, they found him engaged in the meditation of God's Word – the portions being chosen by himself – and rejoicing in Jesus as the only way of salvation. He has since been regular in his attendance at the various prayer meetings held in the town."

Field Meeting

"Yesterday, at three o'clock, one of the most extraordinary and most interesting meetings which has been since the beginning of the movement was held in a spacious field, in front of Eglinton Street. The day being fine, a large number of persons assembled – not less, it is said, than fifteen thousand. About the centre of the field a platform had been improvised on rising ground and here, at the appointed hour, a number of the ministers attending the Wesleyan Conference, which is being held in the town, took their stand. It was a scene not soon to be forgotten. Such a vast multitude of people of every creed in rank and life met together to fill their hearts and voices in praise and prayer to God, and to break the solemn stillness of the Sabbath evening only by the offerings of their worship.

"The method of conducting the service was this – one of the ministers conducted the singing of a hymn, another offered up a prayer, a third read and expounded a portion of scripture, and so on. As the assembly increased in number it was found that the minister's voice could not reach them all, and accordingly another portion of the field was selected where the services were commenced anew and, in a very short time, four immense congregations were grouped in different parts of the field around the ministers.

"In all these meetings the most intense interest and attention were manifested. Everyone seemed to listen as they would to glad tidings from a far country, so engrossed were they, that what fell from the preacher's lips, and when a hymn was read to be sung their voices swelled forth upon the still evening air with peculiar sweetness and impressiveness. The addresses delivered on the occasion were well calculated to arouse the careless and bring conviction to the undecided; and, during the services, many people were led to cry for mercy and pardon through the Saviour's blood, and they were ministered to and prayed over by some of the clergymen in the field, and soon declared that they had found peace by looking unto Jesus."

"The Banner of Ulster" Tuesday, 28th June 1859

Meeting in the Botanic Gardens

"The meeting which will be held tomorrow in the Botanic Gardens has already attracted a vast amount of interest. We understand that about ten thousand tickets have already been distributed. It is suggested that places of business in town should be closed from eleven o'clock 'til the afternoon so as to allow as many as possible to attend the interesting services. A number of the leading establishments have already entered into such an arrangement. Various ministers of the gospel, and converts from Ballymena and other localities, will address the meeting. Mr. Beattie, a Presbyterian gentleman who has been largely instrumental in getting this extraordinary service organised, will himself take part in the proceedings. An expectation was entertained that Brownlow North would be able to attend, but we are not in a position at present to make any positive statement on the subject."

A local Chief Constable on a Case of Revival

"On Friday last, a young woman was stricken down in Donegall Street. The Constable on the beat could not understand her case – she was not drunk, she spoke in a style with which he was not familiar in the course of his official duties and he thought it best to take her, at once, to the Police Office. When she arrived there, however, the Chief Constable (Mr. Lindsay) – the gentleman who discharges his duties with more civility and Christian feeling – at once discovered the state of the young woman's mind. He had her taken into a private room and then placed under the most kindly treatment.

"While in this apartment, the woman burst out into a passionate strain of prayer of the most remarkable character. Mr. Lindsay said that a more beautiful, earnest and impressive prayer he had never before heard. Mr. Lindsay told us that, during the last thirty years, he had been accustomed to all descriptions of impostures, but here he said – to find a young woman, apparently half senseless, deliver herself in such a strain of devotion would be enough to shake the strongest doubter to the effects of the present movement. All of Mr. Lindsay's testimony, with regard to this case, is hardly necessary to go into, but all of it shows that in the case of this young woman there was a most unaccountable evidence of the Spirit of God. For some two or three hours, in his small private room, she sang and prayed; a crowd of course gathered, while she was visited by a minister and, at length, conveyed from the station."

Interesting Incidents of the Work

"Again in Kent Street Schoolroom there have recently been prayer meetings. These have been largely attended, and on Sunday evening there was evidence that the teaching which the audience received was not without its effects. Three manifestations took place during the proceedings, and the people involved were conveyed to their homes in the midst of praise and prayer. In Mary's Place, off Sandy Row, there were also six fresh cases of the power of the Spirit; but so great was the crowd who assembled that we were unable to learn the detailed facts of the cases.

"On Sunday morning one of the members of the Methodist Conference preached in the neighbourhood of Conway Street. There was an immense crowd. During the sermon a young girl, a member of the Roman Catholic community was stricken down. Some of her Roman Catholic neighbours immediately rushed out and threatened to throw buckets of cold water about her if she would continue to show that description of heresy; but the young woman continued notwithstanding these threats to engage in prayer, and was ultimately believing in the Saviour and safely brought home by some friends.

"On Sabbath morning at the early hour of two o'clock a group of young people of both sexes – converts – from Durham Street, Shankill Road, proceeded to visit their brethren and sisters in Christ in Ewart's Row and other neighbouring localities, singing hymns as they went. We were informed that they had been engaged in praise and prayer during the whole of the former part of the night. On Sabbath night, at a late hour, a similar procession had passed down the Shankill Road and suffered no trouble.

"Some very interesting evidence of the first fruits of conversion are furnished by the case of a fine young girl, aged about fifteen years old, who was formerly a Roman Catholic but had listened to the ministry of the Rev. Hugh Hanna for some time before she felt conviction, which is scarcely a week past. She resides with an aunt, who has not yet been visited by the Spirit, and prays fervently and repeatedly that she may be brought to Christ. She declares her intention of devoting all of her available leisure to reading the Bible, praying, praising God and circulating tracts; and she and another girl – also a convert – have actually cleaned out and white-washed an outhouse in a yard belonging to the latter's father as a place for holding prayer meetings with girls like themselves. Through the assistance of some kind friends, this girl has collected a small sum to get tracts and was to make her first purchase last evening."

Conlig

"On Sabbath evening last, Mr. J. M. Porteous lectured in the Rev. S. J. Hanson's church, Conlig, and a collection was taken in aid of the Protestant Institute of Scotland. The church was densely crowded by an attentive audience. In the forenoon of the same day Mr. Hanson preached from the words, 'I have a message from God unto thee.' For the first time on an ordinary Sabbath, both aisles and gallery were crowded. Three cases of conviction occurred – one person cried out in melting tears:– 'Lord Jesus, come quickly.' On the previous Monday evening at a very full meeting, Mr. Workman gave an account of the movement in Belfast.

"The awakening in this neighbourhood commenced on the following night when one of Mr. Hanson's people awoke repeating Isaiah 52:2. On Thursday night Mr. Hanson was aroused to attend to several cases in the village. Little else was heard but cries for mercy from souls under deep distress. After some time one person found peace during the singing of a Psalm, and leaping out of bed she cried:– 'I must pray for Jesus is coming.' After prayer by Mr. Hanson, she appealed most earnestly to her relatives and others, beseeching them to fly to Christ. Another girl on finding peace addressed her friends in forcible terms 'til all were bathed in tears. Another, having obtained mercy, prayed:– 'Let me not turn back into fear but forward into love.'

"In company with Mr. Hanson, Mr. Porteous visited many – both in the village and neighbourhood – and found the sound of prayer and praise issuing from homes where souls were rejoicing in a present Saviour. On this Monday forenoon several others, both male and female, had been found in the depth of conviction. The work is progressing, and the most impressive love is shown by those professing to have found peace, toward each other. This evening another meeting is to be held in the church and to be addressed by a convert from Carrickfergus, and another two are to plead the out-pouring of the Divine Spirit on the district."

Boardmills

"The work progresses very favourably here. On Saturday morning no less than seventy persons, professing deep spiritual concern, waited on the Rev. Mr. Hanks at his own residence. At the prayer meeting the same evening there were many who, after strong conviction, gave evidence of a change of heart and went away, some at a very late hour, rejoicing. On Sabbath evening Professor Gibson addressed an immense audience – the largest ever witnessed in that neighbourhood – in the Rev. Mr. Dobbin's church. So great was the attendance that Rev. Mr. Dobbin had to conduct an extra service at the same time in the adjoining schoolroom. At the close there were many interesting cases, although comparatively few were characterised by any extreme agitation. The movement at Boardmills seems to be, for the most part, calm and solemn. Those who are brought under conviction are speedily emerging into a state of peace and joy. The entire neighbourhood is pervaded by the deepest feeling on the subject and by a general desire to improve the season of gracious visitation."

Ballyeaston

"A correspondent says:– 'I gave you a report until Monday. This week has been nearly equal to our first week. We held five meetings, and in every one we saw the mighty power of God. Thousands attended and very many fell like children to the earth – I should say like Saul of Tarsus – and some of them found peace at once, others were, for more than three hours, groping their way in thick darkness. Yesterday morning, and today, our meetings for prayer at nine o'clock were attended by between four hundred and five hundred souls. A friend addressed them from the Word, and the Lord was pleased to visit many. It was twelve o'clock today before I could leave the house. Even now I cannot finish this note without going to see sin-sick souls, all in the agony of spiritual birth. I hear no sounds from without but songs of praise. Our whole land is shaking from the four winds, O friend.'

"The following are a few extracts from a letter of the Rev. Henry Ormsby, a minister on the Island of Bute, dated Ballyeaston, 21st June:–

"'Sir, I take the liberty to write to you to let you know that I arrived in Ballyeaston last night from Belfast, and was most kindly received by Mrs. Pollock who told me that her husband, the Rev. Mr. Pollock of Ballyeaston, had gone to a meeting at Ballygowan about three miles from Ballyeaston. I went to it and overtook the Rev. Mr. Pollock on the way who very kindly received me and gave me comforting information about the revival. When we arrived at the place of the meeting, which was in a field, I was quite surprised to see hundreds who came flocking over the hills where you could see no houses. It was truly like a moving among the dry bones. There were, I think, nearly two thousand of all ages; there was a great multitude of men; it was a very wet day or there would have been more than there were.

"'The meeting was conducted by the Rev. Mr. Pollock of Ballyeaston, and the Rev. Mr. Whiteford and two young converts from Connor. I can truly say I never saw a more authentic congregation and towards the close, it was beyond all description. The life-giving Spirit of God came down like a mighty rushing wind. There I saw the stalwart men in great agony of soul and body rending the air with their piercing cries for mercy. Here and there through the field I could see the crowd and hear the sound of praise and prayer around someone who had been stricken down, and had been carried away. I never saw such a sight before; may God be pleased to carry it on! Numbers of young women were stricken down. I tried to take notes of the cases, but I could not do so, so great was the power of God among them. We left off near eleven o'clock and had begun at seven o'clock. When we came away the multitude remained in the field. You could hear nothing but cries for mercy, and a great many clasping one another in their arms who had found the peace which passeth all understanding. One band we met were singing the praises of God on the public road. I can only say that the one half was not told to me in Scotland which I now see with my eyes and I cannot put in words what I now see as the power of God.'

"The Banner of Ulster" Thursday, 30th June 1859

Comber

"The good work still continues to progress here. The evening prayer meetings in 'First Comber' are attended by crowds, and awakenings are of daily occurrence. Upwards of two hundred 'cases' in connection with Mr. Killen's congregation have already occurred, and the whole aspect of society is changed. Prayer and praise may be heard in every quarter, the public houses are nearly empty, profanity has ceased and the great topic of conversation is the salvation of the soul. Scoffers have mostly been silenced, and some of them converted.

"Comber Fair on Tuesday presented such an aspect of sobriety, morality and seriousness as was never before witnessed. The Rev. A. Moody Stewart of Edinburgh and the Rev. Milne of Perth visited Comber on Friday last and, in company with Mr. Killen, examined a great many of the awakened and converted with whose condition they seemed greatly solemnised and gratified. They mentioned that they considered the state of matters in Comber much more desirable than anything they had seen in Belfast. Mr. Milne addressed an immense audience in the evening, in Mr. Killen's church. There is to be a large open-air meeting this evening (Thursday) in the Market Square, Comber, at which it is expected ministers from various districts will deliver addresses."

Killinchy

"The gracious awakening, with which the Lord is visiting His people, is making delightful progress in this district. At a prayer meeting on Thursday last, the Divine manifestation appeared in the case of an interesting youth who, when the congregation had partly dispersed, was found bathed in tears, and praying in fervent tones for mercy in Christ. The following evening several were cast down in great agony of soul and, at every meeting since, numbers have been similarly affected who have, afterwards, found great peace and joy in believing.

"On the Sabbath the Presbyterian Church was densely filled, both morning and evening, with a congregation of upwards to fifteen hundred souls. After the usual services, solemn and heart stirring addresses were heard from Mr. Beattie of Ballymena and a current convert from Ahoghill. The quickening power of the Spirit was largely manifested, and the convictions were numerous at both services. A prayer meeting has been held in the same place every evening this week, and the spacious building filled by devout worshippers. The power and presence of the Spirit are witnessed at every meeting. The good work of the Lord is fully begun here and is producing the happiest results in the conviction and conversion of souls. A feeling of deep reverence pervades the whole community, and the Lord is doing wonderful things in righteousness."

"The Banner of Ulster" Saturday, 2nd July 1859

Crossgar

"The great awakening has reached this place. Prayer meetings are held every evening in Lissara Presbyterian Church. At these meetings some have been suddenly convicted, while others have had their hearts gently opened. Many are now rejoicing in Jesus their Saviour. On Thursday evening there was a wonderful display of the grace and power of God. After the meeting was finished, at a late hour, the people seemed unwilling to go to their homes. They still remained within the grounds of the church, and in the open-air prayer after prayer was offered up on behalf of convicted souls. While this was being done some were stricken down, and were heard to say like the publican:– 'God be merciful to me a sinner'. Numbers in this town, who could not be encouraged to attend any place of worship, are found every evening in the sanctuary, and are earnestly praying that they may see Jesus there."

Carryduff

"The blessed work of spiritual revival has been going on here also for the last month. Four weeks ago congregational prayer meetings were begun, which were soon so largely attended that the church could not contain the numbers that thronged to the place of prayer. Although held every evening in the week, there were six hundred to eight hundred present. Beyond the prayer meetings, no means were adapted for exciting the religious feelings of the people. No converts were brought to deliver their soul-stirring addresses, nor were the meetings protracted to a late hour of the night, and yet the Spirit of God has been poured out as abundantly and as effectively as on any other congregation, thus proving that, in a great degree, the work is of God, independent of the work of man.

"The first evidences of the Spirit's work, on the hearts of the people, were seen in many members of the congregation, young and old, coming forward to lead the devotional worship, who had hitherto refused to perform that duty from feelings of shame or incompetence. For three weeks the meetings were conducted entirely by the praying people of the neighbourhood, without any physical displays, until last Sabbath when, during the time the minister was preaching many, like the Philippian jailor, fell down trembling and began to cry out, 'What must I do to be saved?' Every day and night since that time many have been stricken by the Spirit with deep conviction, and have found pardon and peace in the Saviour. One phase of the Spirit's work, in this place, is that nearly all who have been brought under His extraordinary influence are persons advanced in age – some very old – while few young people have yet been struck down. Some curious incidents have also occurred in connection with it here.

"The strangest is that of a woman who belonged to the neighbouring Unitarian congregation, who had never attended one of the prayer meetings, nor any place of worship since they began – who did not believe these revivals to be God's work, but mocked and scoffed at them, and who had never spoken to one of those converted, yet being herself brought under the conviction of sin, and led to cry to Jesus to have mercy on her soul. And, after refusing to see a Unitarian minister, was brought the same evening by her brother, also a Unitarian, to a prayer meeting in Carryduff that she might be instructed and prayed for there. This is done and she has now found both joy and peace in believing.

"Some other remarkable incidents may be noticed – one is that the person who was first struck down by the Spirit declared afterwards that, on the day before, she had gone to her knees in her own house and prayed that she might be the first of the congregation whom the Spirit would visit in this wonderful way, and so it was according to her prayer. A husband and wife were stricken on Tuesday night last in their own house. The husband declared that they might say they had literally prayed without ceasing 'til morning, and they both found comfort in Jesus at the same time. A most respectable woman of the congregation, who was brought deeply under conviction and afterwards found great joy in the Saviour, has been sending for her acquaintances and friends to speak to them of their souls, and afterwards makes them kneel down while she prays with them.

"The following is an incident of one of the fruits of this work and shows plainly the change that has taken place in the minds of the community – a note was delivered without any signature to the treasurer of the congregation two days ago, enclosing a small sum of money as 'restitution' returned as a 'case of conscience under the force of this revival'."

"The Ballymena Observer" Saturday, 2nd July 1859

"With reference to the great work of religious revival, two striking facts are a sample of the much blessed fruit which it has already produced within this town and neighbourhood. First – we can give the names of four young women who five weeks ago were common street prostitutes, and public nuisances in Ballymena, resident in dens of notorious vice, and had been frequently convicted before the local court for drunkenness and 'loitering for the solicitation of customers'. These women are now, in all appearance, thoroughly reclaimed. They are clothed with attention to decency, are struggling to earn their means of livelihood by honest labour, and some of them are learning to read. They are each daily and humbly beseeching pardon from the Almighty for past sin – for grace to strengthen their faith in Jesus Christ, and to support them in the hour of temptation. All are found in regular attendance at some place of public worship every Sabbath day.

"Our second fact is not less striking as an illustration of the prevailing influence, although manifested upon a very different class of the community. There will be no Orange procession in our neighbourhood – no parading with colours, sashes, banners or drums upon the ensuing 12th July. Instead of this, it is intended that the members shall come together in very large crowds, and a number of the Presbyterian clergymen have agreed to preach to them – some in the open-air, and others in their respective churches. To these meetings the people will walk in ranks, but in their ordinary dress, singing hymns of praise to their great 'Spiritual Deliverer'. They will be headed by those who lead their congregational singing. They are, at present, practising tunes for singing Psalms at the event and we found that the favourite tune on the occasion will be that suitable to the 100th Psalm."

Great Union Meeting for Prayer in the Royal Botanic Gardens

"The gentlemen, whom we may term the Directors of this important religious service, were fortunate enough to obtain permission for holding the 'monster meeting' from the committee of the Royal Botanic Gardens, for the use of their beautiful and extensive grounds – the only park which is not private property in the neighbourhood of Belfast, and the only place at all suitable for such a purpose. The centre of the gardens embraces a very spacious lawn, of the smoothest and most velvety grass, particularly encircled by noble elms, beeches and limes, and with scenes contributed in the most tasteful style of artificial landscape, opening in various directions. A more picturesque spot of garden scenery would indeed be difficult to find.

"Commanding the open space we have just described is a spacious and handsome covered platform, resembling the sloping section of an ornamental pavilion, providing seats for about one hundred people. It was from the front of this that the Rev. C. H. Spurgeon, in August last year, addressed the largest audience which ever assembled to hear a minister of the gospel in Ulster. We were present upon the occasion, and remember the extent of ground which the crowd occupied.

"We are therefore, by comparison, enabled to make an approximate estimate of the numbers drawn together to the same place, for a more important object yesterday, and we will not be open to the accusation of overstating them when we calculate them at between four to five times as great a congregation than previously – or, in other words, at between thirty five thousand to forty thousand. We know that about twenty five thousand tickets were issued, and that thousands of people who arrived by special trains on the Ulster, and Ballymena Railways, as well as numbers of others, were admitted without tickets.

"We have heard various figures as to the passengers who reached town, and do not hesitate to say that they must have approached fifteen thousand. The returning train on the Ulster line in the afternoon was the largest, we are informed, that ever left the Belfast terminus. It comprised all the carriages at the company's disposal, and was propelled, at a very moderate rate of speed, by two of their most powerful engines. At least one half of the carriages was so crowded that a considerable proportion of the occupants were seated upon the knees of others, who had earlier obtained places, while others were obliged to content themselves with standing room between the rows. The trains of the Ballymena line were nearly as crowded, but we do not know with certainty the numbers who arrived by this route to be present at the services. We have reason to know, however, that the total was very great.

"A number of those who enjoyed the advantage of the services at the Botanic Gardens found their way by the County Down trains, and by private transport, and many, from short distances in the country, travelled on foot. The leading streets of the town presented, during the midday, a most remarkable aspect particularly after the arrival of trains. The footways were literally thronged with well-dressed, and respectable looking people from the country – not passing along with the casual, and easy-going air of a pleasure-seeking trip, but stayed in a solemn manner – the younger as well as the older, and the majority carried Bibles or hymnbooks in their hands, as if proceeding to Sabbath services.

"On they pressed, towards the point of attraction, past the glittering rows of gorgeous shops, and through the fashionable thoroughfares, unobservant of the style. Thus, the living stream – such a stream as was never before witnessed in Belfast – poured forth, and onwards, for at least two hours, along both sides of the street.

"Long before the hour appointed for the commencement of the proceedings in the gardens, the wide space in the centre of the grounds began to be occupied. Soon the lawn in front of the platform was full, as far as the grand old tree in the middle, and by the opening hour the entire ground, between the pavilion and the conservatory, was completely covered with a dense multitude. The scene, at this period, was certainly one of the most striking, as well as impressive and breathtaking ever witnessed in this province. Crowds, however, continued to pour in through the gates for more than an hour. Consequently, the whole space in view, from any point, was as closely packed as it was possible for it to be.

"Even the branches of the trees were taken advantage of, by numbers of junior members of the audience, as the best positions for seeing and hearing, and there, while the sounds of praise were rising from the multitude below, these young worshippers were heard joining in the song of thanksgiving, the printed words in their hands and the Saviour, it is to be hoped, in their hearts. Nothing of holiday light-heartedness – nothing of the thoughtless hilarity of youth – was seen among them. Their attention to the proceedings was as marked, and their conduct was well behaved, as that of any person in the vast crowd.

"The proceedings of this unparalleled revival meeting commenced at half past eleven. At this time, in the partially shaded enclosure where the platform was situated, there was not a breath of air stirring, and so intense was the expectations, with regard to the service about to be entered upon and their probable results, that every face was anxiously directed towards the Presidential chair. A lengthy silence was broken by the chairman who, in a deeply impressive prayer, implored the outpouring of the Holy Spirit upon those before him. He then read a chapter from the Holy Scriptures and, afterwards, gave out the 100th Psalm, and never before in Belfast did so many voices unite in such hearty singing of this favourite song of Zion. Rarely had the first note been raised on the platform when it was caught up by the immense crowd – the majority of the voices combining in surprising and unexpected harmony.

"The order of the service was as follows – Rev. S. J. Moore (Ballymena) addressed the meeting. Rev. William Johnston offered up a prayer. Mr. J. Francey, of Connor, (a convert), prayed, and delivered an address. The Rev. Hugh Hanna engaged in prayer and also addressed the crowd. The Rev. William Arthur, of London, addressed the meeting. Mr. Bell, of Lisburn, (a convert) offered up prayer, and followed with an address. Dr. Lynn, of Armagh, also addressed the crowd. The Rev. S. M. Dill, of Ballymena, next delivered an address. Mr. Dickson of Broughshane (a convert) offered up a prayer and afterwards gave an address. The Rev. J. Bagley (Independent) delivered an address. Mr. W. J. Cook of Ballymena (convert) – a prayer and an address. Mr. John Montgomery (Portadown) – an address. The Rev. Robert Knox – an address followed by prayer. Mr. William Dickson, elder of the Free Church, Edinburgh – an address. The Rev. S. J. Moore, Ballymena, gave out the popular hymn, 'What's the News?' which was sung with deep feeling, and vigour by the crowd.

"Professor Gibson next delivered an address. Peter Drummond, of Sterling – publisher of the celebrated 'Stirling tracts' – addressed the meeting. The Rev. J. H. Moore, of Connor, prayed and delivered an address. The Rev. Mr. Cather next addressed the crowd. The following verses of a hymn were then sung with much effect to the tune of 'Old Hundredth' –

Just as I am, without one plea,
But that Thy blood was shed for me,
And that Thou bidst me come to Thee,
O Lamb of God, I come! – I come.'

'Just as I am, and waiting not
To rid my soul of one dark blot,
To Thee, Whose blood can cleanse each spot,
O Lamb of God, I come! – I come.'

"The Rev. Mr. Hewitt then offered up prayer, and the proceedings of this long to be remembered day of united devotion were closed with the pronouncing of the benediction by the Moderator.

"It would be evident that many of the crowd were unable to hear the addresses from the platform, on account of the distance at which they were obliged to remain. In order to provide a remedy for this, the Rev. Thomas Toye, the Rev. R. M. Henry, the Rev. Thomas Anderson, the Rev. Mr. Adams and several other ministers with a number of laymen – some of them converts from various distances – scattered themselves among the crowd, each forming the centre of a large congregation which immediately gathered around, and joined in devotional worship. At one time there were no less than twenty of these lesser meetings, numbering from five hundred to one thousand each."

Prayer Meetings of the Young

"One minister was asked to leave the platform to visit several cases of conviction that occurred in the crowd. Eight cases came under his observation and care. In many parts of the garden, the groups of boys and girls, who had retired from the body of the congregation, had formed in the undergrowth little meetings for prayer and exhortation among themselves. Some of these were ragged little boys who had evidently belonged to the outcast classes. They had recently been converted, and several of them prayed in such a manner as to astonish a great many of the most highly educated people in Belfast, who surrounded them.

"One little boy, about eleven years of age, was seized with conviction. He shed numerous tears of repentance, and bewailed the hardness of his heart and the former carelessness of his life, and protested that he would no longer disobey his parents, or refuse to listen to the admonition of his Sabbath School teacher. He said that his sins pressed heavily on his heart, but that he had found the preciousness of the Saviour, and that he would ask the help of God to enable him to cleave to Christ.

"Certain little converts, who had made their way up to the platform through the intervention of Christian friends who knew them, excited a good deal of attention. Ladies and gentlemen who occupied the platform engaged in lengthy conversation with them, and examined them regarding their religious experience and their answers as to their Scriptural knowledge and their experience of the effects of the Divine grace in their hearts. They provided high satisfaction and created great astonishment among the educated bystanders.

"At one of the detached prayer meetings a Sabbath School pupil was heard to pray with eloquence, scripturally and powerfully, which amazed several ministers who were present.

"One of the most interesting incidents was that of a boy eleven years old who, in a very quiet part of the garden, was engaged in prayer surrounded by about twenty lads of the same age and class. This lad, it is known, was neglected by his parents and formerly obtained a scanty livelihood by selling short stories through the streets. Yesterday the tattered garments in which he, as well as his companions, were arrayed, showed that in that respect their prospects in life had not much improved. But this boy commanded the attention of a crowd, at first, numbering about twenty. But afterwards amounting to three or four hundred, with wonderful power. We heard a clergyman, in reference to this prayer state:– 'I was at College five years, have been twenty years a minister of the gospel and, during all that time, I have been unable to approach the Throne of Grace with the beautiful spirit of this mere child.' It may be also remarked that the manner in which the young hearers listened to the service, conducted by their youthful companion, showed the solemn nature of the proceedings.

"At the close of the general meeting one of the ministers of the town, who has moved a great deal among the juvenile population, was surrounded by a large crowd of boys who ultimately formed themselves into a procession, and marched into town singing, 'O, that will be joyful.' Many of these children evidently belonged to the lowest classes of society, and were very poorly clad. But their beaming and happy faces, and the spirit and fervour in which they sang that stirring hymn, demonstrated the very music of their souls. This was one of the most interesting events of the day.

"Not the least remarkable of the scenes witnessed yesterday was that in which a little boy, of about twelve years, was observed going about one of the ornamental ponds, and gathering together a little congregation of children of his age whom he addressed in the most serious manner, telling them how he had been affected. He then commenced to sing a hymn and afterwards prayed in a manner so earnest in style, and beautiful in language, that it brought to tears even grown-up people who heard him. One of them – a Roman Catholic woman – confessed that his words were so overpowering that she was forced to tear herself away.

"The conclusion of the proceedings was as satisfactory, in every way, as those who directed them could have desired. The immense crowd of people left the gardens in a most orderly manner – the majority of them evidently felt, with conviction, that it was good for them to have been there. One thing was confessed by those who were least hopeful as to the result – that the meetings had exceeded expectation in regard to its freedom from unnecessary stirring of emotions."

"The Coleraine Chronicle" Monday, 4th July 1859

"The work of the Lord is in no degree abated in our town and neighbourhood but, on the contrary, increased evidences of the Divine presence have been apparent during the week. The houses of worship belonging to all denominations of Protestants were crowded with the devout and anxious hearers and again, as on a previous Sabbath, God's day of rest was kept, so far as we could see in strict accordance with His Own law. No Sunday drinking was visible and we believe very few availed themselves of the cheap railway fares to visit seaside scenes, which formerly drew crowds of pleasure-seekers from the House of God. The Rev. A. Moody Stewart from Edinburgh, who came over here that he might see and take part in the scenes, preached a very searching sermon in the 1st Presbyterian Church to a very large and very attentive audience. He, with the following clerymen and laymen, and many others, has been on a visit to Coleraine and other places during the week, that he might see with his own eyes, scenes which he read in newspapers that they could scarcely believe.

"On the evenings of Wednesday and Friday large open-air meetings for prayer were held in the new Market Square – at each fully fifteen hundred people were present. The people were addressed by the clergymen of the town. While there was a solemnity and earnestness of manner visible on the faces of the people, no cases of sudden conviction occurred at the meeting, but the seed sown took deep root in the hearts of many and, in the retirement to their own homes that night, several individuals were brought to the Lamb of God. Thus the work is silently progressing and the fruits are abundant and healthy."

"The Belfast Newsletter" Monday morning, 4th July 1859

The Revival in the North

"Journal of the Rev. William Marable, of St. John's, Dublin:– 'Friday morning, half past seven. When waiting for the train at the railway station an old man, seventy two years of age, came up to me named W. B. He was formerly of Broughshane, had been an Arian, and confessed to having carried on a correspondence with the devil. He told me he had been listening to me in the school house the evening before. With tears in his eyes, he said he was very anxious about his soul. He told me he was sure Christ is God; that he greatly liked the prayer I had taught them – 'O, God, for Christ's sake, give me the Holy Spirit!', and had often used it since. His two daughters had been struck in one day, and he was longing to be converted himself. He was now a Presbyterian, and was praying that a Priest L___ might get it.

"'I was informed in the train that in Purple Lane, off Durham Street, opposite Christ Church, Belfast, as many as fifteen people were convicted in the course of two days in one girl's house; that three Roman Catholics were convicted at one time in Belfast. The Priest visited them, looked at two of them, and went away, and said of a third, 'She has had too much drink', and left. There were two cases of mill girls (Roman Catholics) who pretended to be stricken, and began to pray after a Roman Catholic fashion; they were afterwards really struck down, and are now Bible-reading Christians. The Priests are utterly confounded.

"'A lady in a train (Mrs. W. C. of C. Street, Belfast) informed me of many interesting cases of Unitarians being converted in Belfast. One young man, a Unitarian who lived next door to her – the brother of a Unitarian minister and one whom she knew intimately – is now doing all he can to propagate the truth. On Wednesday week last he, with another young man, went up the Falls Road (where there are

five or six factories) distributing tracts. All were well received with
the exception of two Roman Catholic girls who were sitting on the
steps at a door. One of these girls was more violent than the other.
She tore up the tracts and put them under her feet, and tried to
snatch the others out of his hand, rebuked him for interfering with
Roman Catholics – that they did not interfere with others, and she
became very abusive indeed. The young man said a few kind words
and went on distributing the remainder of the tracts. On returning
he saw a great many people about the door where these girls had been
sitting. He went in and found one of the girls crying for mercy, and
especially exclaiming:– 'O my sin, my sin, which I have committed in
acting so to these young men!'

"'I proceeded to the Giant's Causeway. The driver of the car told me
of several cases that he knew of conviction, especially of a strong
young woman, a Roman Catholic, who was suffering great
persecution for not going to Mass and attending the Protestant
meetings, but that she was braving it well and not suffering anything
to hinder her in serving God. This driver was very anxious about his
own soul, and told me he knew of a meeting in a village nearby where
fifty people had been convicted in one evening. The guide I engaged,
Joseph K. of Bushmills, was very anxious on the subject of religion
and had great desire to be converted, but said he felt he was not, as
yet, the Lord's.

"'On reaching the hotel at the Giant's Causeway, seeing I was a
clergyman, all the guides, both men, servants, and peasants, gathered
to me and I preached to them in the open-air on the rising ground
behind the hotel. The hotel keeper, a widowed lady, came out with
others, for half an hour and I addressed them. Nothing could exceed
the marked solemnity and attention that prevailed; they thanked me
much afterwards. These people are generally the torment of visitors,
but were now intent to listen to 'the Good News' I was privileged to

address to them. Afterwards I addressed some others who seemed deeply impressed.

"'A Unitarian lady and gentleman travelled back to Portrush in the same car with me, and I took care to inform them regarding the present movement. The gentleman acknowledged that the efforts proved abiding and that it is a wonderful work. At Portrush I called on the Curate, Rev. F.; he brought me to visit three cases of conviction. I heard of others. He told me of one place in County Down where, on the last fair day, not a single drunken person was to be seen. While the train stopped ten minutes at Coleraine, a young man told me that the Rev. John C. in K., who lives near Ballymoney, went to see the revival there and was stricken himself, while at tea. The Rector of Ballymoney, Mr. P. is, I understand, an altered man.

"'Two Roman Catholic converts from Ballymoney, aged about twenty, Mr. C. and N., had addressed a meeting in Portrush lately at which some were convicted. There had been over one hundred cases in Coleraine. A Presbyterian clergyman in the railway told me that he knew one case of conversion, and that seven devils had been cast out of the woman – a greater change could not have been apparent. He also said that the days we live in are like the Apostolic times; that in all his ministerial experience (of eight years), he had never seen so many tears shed, so many prayers offered, such cries for mercy, and so many open Bibles, as he has witnessed within the last three weeks in Belfast.

"He mentioned a case of a woman with very bad character, who had been converted in Bushmills. Also, of a Roman Catholic swearer, who could never speak without taking an oath, being stricken and now so altered he has never since been heard to utter a curse. He also assured me that any minister speaking discourteously of this movement is despised by the people. Several Unitarians lately walked out of a Unitarian meeting house at Ballyclare, a place ten miles north-east of Belfast, while Mr. H., their minister, was denouncing the revival. The Unitarian ministers, in general, are more bitter against the movement than the Roman Catholic Priests.

"'At the same place (Ballyclare), a Presbyterian asked a Unitarian what he thought of this work, as they met at one of the monster meetings, where some thousands assembled. The Unitarian asked, 'Well, what do you think of it?' He said, 'I think the Hand of God is in it, but what do you think of it?' 'Well,' said the Unitarian, pointing to a little girl who was just then praying with conviction, 'What can I think of it when that is my own child who is thus praying?' Three brothers (car drivers), all of them very wild, were influenced. A person asked one of them, who was very much changed, 'What will you do about driving cars on Sunday?' His reply was, 'God will provide for me and I will work for Him.'

"'This clergyman mentioned two most remarkable instances of the resource of prayer – in the case of an ignorant man, and of a working girl. He had never heard anything like it. Those stricken down usually cry out as follows – 'Lord Jesus, have mercy on my soul!' 'Lord Jesus! Come to me; come quickly! Have mercy on my soul! O my sins are there! I see them! I see them! O Lord Jesus, have mercy! Have mercy!' And, after a short time, they generally begin to pray silently and call out, 'Sing a Psalm', which calms them.

"'Mr. M. informed me, when I returned to Ballymena, of the case of a woman who had separated from her husband, in consequence of her violent temper; she was convicted, and afterwards went to a woman whose character she had openly attacked in the street, and knelt down to ask her pardon. The woman was so affected that they were clasped in each other's arms.

"'A man by the name of Mr. L., a public housekeeper, was struck about three weeks ago, and was quite contorted in body, and his face became so livid that he was almost bursting. People thought that he was in a fit of apoplexy. He was found with clenched hands for some time crying for mercy. He has now closed his public house, pulled down the signboard and cast it into the backyard, and is a most exemplary Christian.

"'Visited B., in Ballymoney Street, whose daughters had been Unitarians, and converted. They were out. Met there C., a converted man, who said, 'I hope, Sir, you will carry the spark with you to Dublin.' He had been more than a week going about praying with the people and not getting more than an hour's rest each night, so busily engaged was he in this work. I attended Mr. M's meeting house; it was crowded. Many of the Sidney Lane bad women were there. F., a humble man, a stone breaker who could not read six months ago, and was converted in Connor, where the first work commenced a year before, addressed the meeting in the most earnest and fluent terms, reading the account of the Philippian jailor and commenting on it. His prayer also was very spiritual and good. This man had been so great a drunkard that he had to be tied with ropes, when in that condition.

"'The meeting broke up at eleven o'clock. On my way to the hotel I spoke to several at a corner of a street, and begged of them to remember Dublin in their prayers. Even at that late hour they seemed willing to remain and hear something more for their souls' profit, but I did not think it right to detain them. I was sorry to hear, that day, that a Presbyterian clergyman at C. was out of his mind with overwork. Mr. H. had preached again in Sidney Lane to the abandoned characters there, some with tears in their eyes. He told them that if the Lord Jesus were now on earth, the spot He would choose to preach in would be where he then was; that such was His love, when in the world, He proclaimed salvation even to the very worst of sinners. This, in particular, seemed to affect them.

"'The Priests in Ballymena have their chapel open two or three times a day, to try to keep the people from attending the prayer meetings. On arriving in Belfast, I visited for three hours in Sandy Row and the neighbourhood; all the stricken cases I saw (about a dozen) had been affected, more or less, in the same manner and were all happy and reformed in life. I was particularly struck with the last case. Nancy C., not eighteen years of age was living in C. Street. I shall not attempt to describe this scene or the words she uttered but, when in half an hour she awoke out of the trance and became reconciled to see so many faces looking in amazement at her, and the tears flowing from all eyes, her tongue, which could scarcely articulate plainly before, became loosened and, in the most eloquent manner, she addressed all present (especially an old man weeping at the foot of the bed), on the subject of salvation, with an impression of holy joy and gratitude, and an intense love beaming in her intelligent countenance. She, in the middle of her address, called on us to sing a hymn, 'O! That will be joyful', and continued for several minutes in such eloquent strains that all present were compelled to admit they had never seen or heard anything like it before. I would, myself, have gone a thousand miles to see this one case. I did not think it possible that the human countenance could be lit up with so sweet and happy an expression of delight, while she testified of the love of Jesus and of her love for Him.'"

"The Banner of Ulster" Thursday, 7th July 1859

Brownlow North

"On last Sabbath this distinguished evangelist preached in the afternoon at Rosemary Street and in the evening at May Street Church. Although these services had not been very extensively announced, long before the preacher appeared both churches were entirely filled with the most respectable and intelligent audience. We understand that, in the morning Dr. Morgan made a special mention of Mr. North and the remarkable story of his life, and that the Fisherwick Place Church was closed in the afternoon in order that both minister and people might have the opportunity of hearing the distinguished stranger.

"At half past one, Mr. North ascended the pulpit and proceeded to give out the 40th Psalm interspersing the reading of it with explanatory and exhortatory remarks. After a very fervent prayer the first chapter of the Gospel according to John was read and illustrated by several most pertinent and striking observations. The text selected was – 'Christ hath redeemed us from the curse of the law, being made a curse for us', upon which, for about forty minutes the preacher addressed the congregation with uncommon energy and effect. There is something in Mr. North's appearance which, at once, arrests attention. He is middle height and full figure. His features are large and striking, and his eyes are clear and penetrating. His voice is full toned and rich, which he can employ with great power and little apparent exertion, while he seems to possess words at will. The chief feature of the speaker's manner is his earnestness.

"His first and chief object appears to be to convince sinners of the reality of the two persons, God and Satan. He strives to make men really believe and feel conscious that Jesus Christ is beside them everywhere – that He hears every word they say, just as surely as they know that they hear themselves. The practical unfaithfulness of so many multitudes is one of the most convincing proofs of our natural depravity. If men, who profess to believe in the existence of God, believed indeed that He was beside them every day and knew every thought of their heart, every word of their mouth, and every action of their life, would they live as they do? An immense step has been gained by the sinner, when he is enabled to realise the actual existence of God.

"This was very strikingly illustrated in Mr. North's own experience. The gaining of this knowledge cost him the most severe and protracted struggles, and yet he had always nominally believed in God and Satan, Heaven and Hell. One peculiarity of the preacher's style is the worship, and he constantly adds explanatory remarks. He says that men have the habit of engaging in these parts of public worship without giving thought to what they are doing, and out of this deplorable and criminal laziness it is his constant object to arouse them. Just before dismissing the congregation on the Sabbath, Mr. North made renewed appeals to their consciences and sent them away most deeply impressed with the solemn and all important truth so plainly and forcibly urged upon them. We have never heard the inexcusable folly of the unconverted sinner so clearly demonstrated, or the awful guilt which he incurs by his neglect of salvation so powerfully depicted."

"The Banner of Ulster" Saturday, 9th July 1859

Children's Meeting

"There was held this week in Berry Street Church, at midday, a meeting for children. The attendance numbered about three hundred young people and there were probably about a third of them who had been awakened to a sense of sin and had found peace in Christ. Two of the boys, both in very poor attire – one of them barefooted – prayed. They were barely able to read their Bibles; they poured out their souls before God with a fervency that the Spirit of God alone can kindle in the heart."

A Happy Result of the Revival

"A young man driving a bread cart down Durham Street, the scene of last year's unhappy party political excitement, was, a couple of days ago, silly enough to exhibit an orange lily on the horse's head. This very foolish act would formerly, of course, have created a tumult in the neighbourhood. A very different result followed on this occasion. A number of young lads (Protestant converts) standing at a corner, seeing the driver pass, consulted as to the proper means of putting a stop to the party political exhibition. Two of their number were sent to follow him to the first shop at which he might stop. There they kindly remonstrated with him as to the foolishness of displaying the obnoxious emblem, asking him to have the goodness to remove it, with which request he, at once, complied."

Claggin, Near Cookstown

"In this congregation, for some time past, the work of the Lord has been making hopeful progress. A good number, after weeks perhaps months of deep conviction, are now rejoicing in Jesus. Many deeply wounded spirits are still labouring under the heavy burden of sin and can get no rest 'til the blood be applied, and the curse be removed, and peace be enjoyed. One small meeting for prayer, in a farmer's house, we must notice. After praise and short prayers from two or three whose hearts the Lord had touched, and after a portion of scripture had been read and simply applied, those under a deep sense of sin were requested to wait for consultation.

"Upwards of a dozen complied with the request. Their difficulties were made known to each other and a few words were spoken by one who had personal experience in similar circumstances. The small company then kneeled together with one accord at the Throne of Grace. A short prayer was offered, but no one moved. This sweet worship continued 'til nearly everyone present felt the power of the mighty Spirit. Some, after a short mental agony, were enabled to rejoice in Jesus, while others were either completely prostrated or, with all the powers of mind and body, were pouring forth that deep piercing cry to Heaven:— 'Jesus come! Come quickly! And break my chains! Take all my sins away! Save me now!' Others returning from the meeting or to their homes were impressed. One poor girl who had no closet for private prayer, chose the bedside to pour out the burden of her soul to God. There she was visited and there she lay 'til her cries for mercy brought her friends to her humble Bethel. The night was passed in deep distress but the morning brought sweet peace in Jesus."

"The Banner of Ulster" Tuesday, 12ᵗʰ July 1859

Berry Street Church

"The attendance in this church overflows at all the meetings. Hundreds were unable at both services on the Sabbath to obtain admittance. The physical manifestations are not so numerous, but the number of anxious enquirers is multiplying and conversions obtained through silent struggles of the soul are greatly increasing. The work is deepening and extending and gives tokens of a very satisfactory character. On Sabbath morning last the prayer meeting filled the lower part of the church. The meeting was refreshing. The Sabbath Schools now fill the church. There is not room for another class in the building or the adjacent rooms. Yesterday evening there was held a meeting of the visitors and converts. A few strangers, who were on a visit to witness the work of the Lord, were admitted. The church was filled. Several most interesting cases of conviction occurred.

"A very intelligent though an uneducated Roman Catholic girl, who fled from her mother's house to escape persecution, has turned up. The Priest was brought to her but she refused to have any discussion with him, on any subject. She effectively repulsed him, and sought Protestant protection that she may enjoy her conviction of truth and follow her dictates of duty. Another Roman Catholic girl of very considerable intelligence was challenged by her friends to meet the Priest. She accepted it, and trampled over the teachings of Rome. Her faith has received confirmation from the encounter. Two other cases of the conversion of Romanists were reported by the visitors. The Lord is shaking anti-Christ. Every day reveals some new and startling facts that demonstrate the work to be of God and call on a grateful Church to recognise and acknowledge the goings on of the Lord."

Saintfield

"We are happy to be informed that the good work is still going on in Saintfield.   The meetings for prayer held each week in the Presbyterian churches alternately, are still largely attended, and every night there have been cases of conviction of sin. Several young men and young women have been stricken down and heard to cry for mercy. Some old men are also now rejoicing in Christ Jesus. All undue excitement is discouraged and all are cautioned against mistaking conviction for conversion. Family worship is now established in many families where it was previously unknown. One of the most cheering sounds which a man could hear is the singing of Psalms by the different groups of people going to their own homes after the prayer meeting closes.

"The whole face of the country is changed. Drunkenness has, to a large extent, ceased. One publican has given up his trade and others are about to follow his example. Would if some of those ministers of the Church of England, who appear to be opposing this movement, could hear the language and the prayers of some of the people! It would lead them to change their views and, if they will not aid the work, at least lead them to speak more charitably concerning it. The other evening the people were warned against the statements of such men as Mr. McWayne and asked to pray for them, that the Lord might lead them to change their views of the work and lead them to think more seriously of the use which Romanists and others are making of their foolish and unguarded statements."

"The Banner of Ulster" Saturday, 16th July 1859

"A great number of ministers, elders and lay gentlemen from Scotland and England have been visiting amongst us for a number of days, their sole object being to ascertain the real state of revivals here. Our friends from Scotland, with a caution and insight characteristic of their country, have been making the most detailed enquiries. Amongst other things they have ascertained that, in almost every case which they have visited, there had been a looking and praying for conversion for longer or shorter periods. In fact, that a work of the Spirit had been going on long before there was the sudden conviction or the striking down in some cases. There is no doubt that they will enlighten their countrymen as to the true nature of the present great work, many of whom seem to think that people here fall down without ever having had a serious thought upon the subject of religion. Yesterday morning the Glasgow Steamer brought a considerable addition to the number of our visitors. Several of the gentlemen are from Dundee."

Lecumpher

"Since our last notice we understand from a correspondent that the work of revival has been making rapid progress in this locality, and that many cases of conviction have taken place, some of which are of the most interesting kind. On the last Sabbath an evening service was held at this church but, when the hour to commence arrived, it was found necessary to hold it in the open-air on the Meeting House green.

"There were five or six Roman Catholics present, one of whom, a strong, old soldier of the 29th Regiment, distinguished in India, was seen retiring from the green and, after a few paces, he staggered and fell on the roadside where he was found at the close of the service. He was carried back to the green where he remained attended by Mr. Wilson and a few others, 'til a late hour. He was kindly brought into the house of a respectable and godly farmer for whom he had laboured and who, with a few others, sat up with him during his agonising daze, 'til early next morning when for the first time he cried out, 'God have mercy upon my soul! Lord save me!' And then asked for the Bible, and requested his employer to read and pray with him. This being done, he asked for the Bible again, and clasped it to his breast saying, 'This is the Word of God.'

"On Monday he was visited by Mr. Wilson to whom he related his past history, confessing himself a great sinner, especially as a blasphemer. He was presented with a Testament and, though unable to read, it is pleasing to see this man resume his labours, sitting and spelling word by word the precious gospel. Having renounced at once all connection with popery he attended the prayer meeting at Lecumpher on Wednesday and promises attendance at the worship of God in that place for the future. His wife, though still a Roman Catholic, rejoices at the change already visible in him. For the last four days crowded prayer meetings have been held at which several have been smitten down, while others are affected on their way home, or in their own houses. It is worthy of notice that the Roman Catholic above referred to was often seen standing behind a hedge under the open-air preaching of last summer in this neighbourhood but is now not ashamed to be seen on his knees in prayer, both at home and in the Presbyterian church ."

"The Ballymena Observer" Saturday, 16ᵗʰ July 1859

"One of the most remarkable and hopeful characteristics of the religious movement was displayed throughout the greater portion of County Antrim and, more especially so, in Ballymena and the adjoining districts on Tuesday last being the anniversary of King William's glorious and important victory at the Boyne. We were aware that the Orangemen, at this part of the county, had resolved to observe the day as one of thanksgiving to God for the providential setting up and maintenance of that civil and religious freedom, which all subjects of the realm – Roman Catholics, as well as Protestants – now so happily enjoy.

"We knew the Orangemen of the district well enough to feel persuaded that their resolution would be carried into effect, but we feel happy in saying that our most optimistic anticipations have been more than achieved by their excellent conduct on the occasion, and by the tranquillity, self-denial, devotional manner, and perfect unity of their proceedings.

"In accordance with previous arrangements, an open-air meeting for united prayer was held at one o'clock, on a grass park in the vicinity of the town. The day was beautifully fine and, at the appointed hour, every thoroughfare leading to the spot was crowded with Orangemen. It was a quiet and solemn occasion – without banners, ribbons, drums or music. We saw thousands of Bibles – for almost every individual present at the meeting was provided with a copy of the Sacred Volume. We did not hear a cheer, an oath, a party expression, nor an angry word at any hour of the entire day. On a modern estimate the number assembled within the field was about six thousand, and the adjoining road was covered and the ditches surmounted, by many additional spectators.

"The chairman was John Jellett, who addressed a few words of congratulations to the audience on the subject of their commendable conduct. After which the Rev. Daniel Mooney opened the religious service with a solemn and appropriate prayer. The Rev. William Davison, Presbyterian minister of Cloughwater congregation, then addressed the audience. He characterised the meeting as one of the most glorious that had ever assembled in commemoration of the victory at the Boyne. They had come there not heralded by pipe and drum, nor marching under the banners of an institution to which they were, no doubt, very attached – they had come with the Bible in their hands, and he also trusted with its teaching written upon their hearts, and under the glorious banner of their faith they would go forth to the battle of the Lord. After an eloquent sermon, wherein he mentioned the prevailing religious movement as the work of God for the conversion of many souls to righteousness, he included an earnest exhortation to peace, charity and unity, and to a godly walk and conversation as the fruits of their faith in Christ, and the best evidence of their conversion.

"The Rev. A. Gault of Cushendall then addressed the meeting. He selected for the subject of his observations the 2nd chapter of First Peter from the 7th verse. With a powerful discourse he exhorted the audience to watchfulness lest they should give occasion to the enemies of God to blaspheme. He bore testimony to the reality and importance of the great religious movement now extending so rapidly throughout the North, and concluded with some appropriate observations on the liberty of conscience – the peace, the tranquillity and freedom which we now enjoy.

"After a few remarks from the Rev. J. Meade Hobson, of Kilkenny, who warmly congratulated the audience on the proceedings of that glorious day and on the blessed change now in progress over this portion of the kingdom, the Rev. Mr. Mooney read, without comment, the 55th chapter of Isaiah as a proper close of the proceedings. The entire audience then sung the National Anthem, after which the Rev. Mr. Gault pronounced the benediction and at four o'clock the members of the Orange Institution left the field in the same quiet and orderly manner in which they had entered. About two thousand people of the neighbourhood remained, and were occupied in religious worship until nine o'clock.

"In the evening, the Rev. Mr. Rossborough, of Glasgow, conducted a divine service in the First Presbyterian Church, and the Rev. Messrs. Gault and Hobson addressed a crowded congregation in the Parochial School. There was not a single arrest for drunkenness, nor any reported charge of drunkenness made in Ballymena during the entire day or the following night. Empty cells are easily guarded, and the governor of our Bridewell had a holiday! So ended the Orange anniversary in Ballymena.

"The Police reports from every district of the county tell of public tranquillity. The united prayer meetings at Randalstown were attended by about six thousand Orangemen of that district. Not one of them appeared with the slightest emblem of the brotherhood, and all was peace. In Buckna the Rev. S. Hamilton conducted a divine service at an open-air meeting attended by many thousand brethren of that neighbourhood, who appeared in their ordinary dress and proceeded to the meeting singing Psalms of praise and thanksgiving along the way. At Ballyscullion Grange, the Rev. Mr. Denham and other ministers preached to an open-air crowd of about two thousand.

"The First Presbyterian Church of Ahoghill, and the Second of Portglenone, were open for a divine service, and excellent sermons were preached by the Rev. D. Adams and the Rev. James Knox. A revival discourse was also preached at the Parish church of Portglenone by the Rev. Mr. Warren, and on every occasion the services were conducted with the greatest order and gravity. An open-air meeting, very well attended, was held at Rasharkin and houses of public worship were opened for divine worship and filled with crowded congregations in almost every district relating to this portion of the county.

"In connection with this subject, we feel great pleasure in reprinting the following very gratifying communication from a godly and distinguished clergyman of the Presbyterian Church:– 'On the 12th July at Loan, near Ahoghill, in a field of Mr. John Ballagh, a union prayer meeting was held at twelve o'clock. It was deeply solemn and heart-inspiring to witness several Orange lodges marching to the field, not as before to sound of pipe and drum but with grave, sweet melody singing the praise of God. It was calculated that about six thousand people were present on the occasion. The weather was all that could be desired.

"Instead of political and inflaming lectures, very solemn and deeply interesting religious services were conducted by the Revs. Gass, Cowan and Buick, and Mr. A. Hutton. The audience was very solemn. Many convictions took place during the day. The Lord was in the midst, doing His mighty work. Around the field and in the adjoining ground, many groups were collected singing praises and ministering to the comfort of the spiritually distressed. A collection was taken up for procuring Bibles and clothes for the poor. At six o'clock the benediction was pronounced, and the vast crowd quietly dispersed – confessing one to the other that they never had spent such a 12th July as before.

"Order and earnestness, and prayer and praise, the reading and the preaching of the Word were the great characteristics of the day. There was no drinking, no disorder, no provoking words, no offensive conduct. This is a glorious change. It is the work of God. It is a delightful result of this gracious revival. Blessed be God, the welcome shower of Divine Grace is still falling abundantly on this entire district."

"Banner of Ulster" Saturday, 16th July 1859

The Twelfth of July at Dundrod

"Nothing could better prove the complete and happy change that has taken place in this district within the last month, in the manner in which the anniversary of Tuesday last was observed. It is unnecessary to state how it was kept in former years. The last 12th, however, was observed not as a holiday, but as a holy day – as a solemn Sabbath, which commenced, continued and ended in praise, prayer and other religious worship.

"In the forenoon, the brethren who met in Dundrod came to the hall with their Bibles in their hands, and waited on Mr. McGill with the request that he would go to their place of meeting and engage in religious worship with them and others assembled. This request was cheerfully complied with. In the evening, by special request, a prayer meeting was held in Dundrod at six o'clock. The Orangemen from the surrounding district came in great numbers, without either music, banners or any party badge. They arrived as solemn, serious men going up to worship God in His sanctuary.

"They had nothing to distinguish them as Protestants but their Bibles, which they carried in their hands. The numbers assembled were so great that the large church could not hold them, and the meeting was held in the open-air, in an enclosed garden in the rear of a schoolhouse. The greatest order, solemn and deep seriousness prevailed during the whole service, which lasted about two hours among the vast assembly of about twelve hundred men.

"The people afterwards, who separated, went home in groups wondering at the strange 'twelfth' they had witnessed, and blessing God for the privilege and pleasure enjoyed throughout the day. Not an oath, not an insulting word, not a party expression issued from the lips of man or woman was seen or heard throughout the whole day. In the middle of the day Mr. Smyth, the Rector of Glenavy, and his two curates, conducted a religious service to a large crowd in a field at Knockcairn, about two miles from Dundrod. The attendance was large, orderly and very attentive."

"The Ballymena Observer" Wednesday, 20ᵗʰ July 1859

"From Ballycastle we learned, on the authority of a respectable correspondent, that many Roman Catholics had been brought under the awakening influence of God's Spirit in their own houses, and the evidence of their conversion will shortly appear in their public withdrawal from all connection with the Church of Rome.

"We may also remark that on Tuesday last, in an area within two miles of Ballymena, the daughter of a man well known as a bigoted Roman Catholic was suddenly, and very deeply 'convicted' while in her father's house. An astonished parent witnessing her strange condition and hearing her fervent prayers to the Saviour on her own behalf, and for the extension of Divine Grace and mercy to himself, and to other members of his family, was forced impulsively to exclaim, 'I cannot resist this demonstration of Almighty power! Truly this must be the work of God!'

"The Banner of Ulster" Tuesday, 26th July 1859

Castlederg, County Tyrone

"A correspondent states the following:– 'I am glad to inform you that the Lord has, in answer to prayer, poured out His Spirit abundantly upon the people of this neighbourhood. On Sunday 10th July 1859, two young men from Londonderry, Messrs. Dickson and Patton, and Reverends Love, Armstrong and Crocket, Presbyterian ministers of Castlederg and neighbourhood, and also Dr. Motherwell, and Rev. Sir Dugan, Wesleyan minister of Castlederg addressed about two thousand five hundred people at five o'clock in the evening in Dr. Motherwell's field, adjacent to Castlederg bridge, on the all important subject of the soul's salvation, calling upon all the people to prepare to meet their God.

"Though there were not many public external manifestations of bodily prostration, all appeared to be deeply concerned and some told me afterwards that they left the meeting praying and that they continued all night in prayer to God for mercy. On Sunday 17th Mr. Donnelly and young men from Londonderry addressed congregations at Rev. Love's Meeting House and also at Rev. Crocket's, and in the Wesleyan Chapel at noon. Afterwards they led the ministers of the town and neighbourhood as on the previous Sunday at five o'clock when there was over four thousand of a congregation.

"Mr. Donnelly addressed the meeting in a very solemn manner, which had a visible effect on all present, and after him, while Mr. Dunne was singing the first two lines of a hymn in which all the congregation joined, a strong man was stricken down and on his removal there was one of the most uncommon manifestations of the Divine presence that was ever witnessed by me in any place – either in the Botanic Gardens, or in any other place in Belfast or elsewhere – since the commencement of this great revival. The young men from Londonderry also said they saw nothing so great. It was like what Isaiah saw – the whole house was filled with His glory; the singing had to cease because there was nothing through the crowd but sobbing and sighing – some calling for mercy, others rejoicing in a sin-pardoning God. The Lord was present in His mighty power. The scene was such that no mortal pen could describe – it was one long to be remembered and, I am convinced, it will be remembered with gratitude and praise by many and, I hope, by all then present through the countless ages of eternity.

"At a late hour Mr. Dunne, with great difficulty, got the crowded congregation dismissed even after pronouncing the benediction six times. Some found peace having believed in Jesus and were, subsequently, enabled to rejoice with joy unspeakable and full of glory, others had to leave with their friends crying unto the Lord Jesus to have mercy upon them. To attempt to give a correct number of those stricken down and who were weeping and calling for mercy would be utterly impossible. The feeling was so general in the crowded house.

"About half an hour after the congregation was dismissed two young men came to our house telling us there were three persons stricken down on the road going home, between twelve and one o'clock, opposite the Rev. Mr. Edwards' house, the Rector of the Parish. Mr. Donnelly, Mr. McLean and myself with some others found, as was told to us, the persons lying on the ground calling on the Lord Jesus to have mercy on them and enquiring what they must do to be saved. Their cries were heart-rending. One person was afraid of going one step further, and asked, 'Do you not see that terrible gulf before me?' We, with some difficulty, got them removed to Mr. Johnston's house where we were hospitably received and, after continuing for nearly an hour in prayer and singing, one of them acknowledged to have found peace in believing – and began to point out to the others Jesus and Him crucified.

"As we were exhausted by the labours of the day, we had to leave and I visited some of these people during the next day. Some had found peace and others were still calling for mercy. As all the cases above described were living in the same townland, I established a weekly prayer meeting in that area and invited them to attend the union prayer meeting in the Wesleyan Chapel on Tuesday evening. At the union prayer meeting on Tuesday evening at seven o'clock, Mr. Dunne, the Wesleyan minister, gave a very interesting account of what he saw and felt lately, when in Belfast at Botanic Gardens and in Sandy Row and elsewhere, which was delivered in that interesting and emphatic earnest and practical style for which that popular preacher is so much distinguished. So you see the Lord's work is reviving all around, from the lowest parts of Down to the most northern parts of County Tyrone. And I heard today from a friend in Ballybofey, in County Donegal, the Lord is doing a great work there also and in Castlefin."

"The Ballymena Observer" Friday, 29th July 1859

Persecution of a Convert

"We have today to observe a remarkable case of conversion in the person of an intelligent Roman Catholic, residing in the eastern division of the borough, which certainly deserves Protestant sympathy. Her sister had been brought to the knowledge of the truth by attending a meeting in the Rev. Hugh Hanna's church. The girl was warned that if she went to see her, six months penance would be imposed upon her by the Priest. She replied that she did not care about that, visited her sister and, afterwards, was struck with conviction when visiting an acquaintance. She was taken home, and remained in a state of physical prostration for a considerable time.

"After her recovery she was smitten down a second time and sent for the Rev. Mr. Roe but her Roman Catholic neighbours would not point out her residence to him. She afterwards sent for the Rev. H. Hanna who had difficulty in finding the house, from the same cause. After being prayed with, and exhorted, she found peace in Jesus and remained steadfast amidst relentless and heartless persecution. She is assailed in the streets with laughter and mockery. Her windows were broken while her little brothers were in bed, narrowly escaping serious injury, if not death, from bricks thrown in.

"Whilst she was ill, three rude young fellows, Roman Catholics half-intoxicated, entered into the house and annoyed her very much by their rough conversation, and soiled her Bible. They brought in whiskey, drank it, went out and reported that she had drunk some, and had been 'revived' – which was a falsehood. So great did the annoyance become that she was forced to claim the protection of the police who, we hope, will prevent her from being further molested."

"The Banner of Ulster" Tuesday, 2nd August 1859

Movement Among the Outcasts

"Of the many notable effects of the Spirit's work, which we have to chronicle from time to time, the most astounding are these which it is our duty to notice today as among the latest. The light has begun to dawn in the darkest and most degraded spots within our civic boundaries. In the neighbourhood of the infantry barracks exists a network of low and miserable streets, lanes and courts, inhabited by a class of persons with the most immoral character. Among these places are the infamous Walker's Lane and the localities adjoining. Cases of disorderly conduct have been, for some time, partly on the decrease there and the Constabulary of North Queen Street Station, as well as the local Police, began to feel somewhat surprised at this.

"On Saturday evening, however, a number of the unfortunate females in those lanes left their old haunts of vice and professed a desire to become reformed in character and conduct. Seven or eight of them were received into the house of a charitably-minded woman, residing in Hardinge Street, where some praying people remained with them, advising them and endeavouring to lead them not only to reform their lives but to 'repent and be converted.' There are about a dozen others in the same lanes all desirous of changing their mode of life, and steps are being taken to send them into places of industrial employment. Others have been sent home to the country. Some outcasts are anxious to get employment in the mills, or elsewhere, so they may earn a livelihood, but all of them gave evidence of a sincere desire to forsake their evil ways and lead a better life in the future. A person who kept one of these dens of vice in Walker's Lane has closed it up and she, along with the other inhabitants are following the path of the repentant. On Sabbath night, 'til the late hour, religious services were conducted in a house in that wretched quarter, where no sound or thought of holiness found entrance or utterance before."

"The Banner of Ulster" Thursday, 4th August 1859

Dromara

"The good work has, at length, extended to this Parish and has come with marvellous power. For some time past joint prayer meetings have been held in the 1st and 2nd Presbyterian Churches which, on different occasions, were addressed by the Rev. J. J. Black of Dublin, by converts from Ahoghill, and others. On the 25th the joint meeting was held in Mr. Craig's church, and was addressed by Messrs. Workman and Lee from Belfast. On the way home from it seven people were smitten down under conviction. On the 29th another meeting, consisting of about two thousand people, was held in the green beside Mr. Patton's church which was addressed by Dr. Steen and two converts from Connor. During the evening and the next day not fewer than fifty or sixty people were convicted of sin. Another meeting, even larger than the preceding, was held last Sabbath evening in the same place and was addressed by Messrs. W. and A. Wilson of Saintfield. On that evening, and since, between one hundred and two hundred people, as far as can be known, were led to cry out, 'What must I do to be saved?' The whole Parish is in a wonderful state of excitement, there being little else done than singing, reading, and praying."

"The Ballymena Observer" Saturday, 6th August 1859

"We regret to state that the good conduct of the intelligent Roman Catholics of Kells, in reference to the revival movement, has not been imitated by their co-religionists in County Derry. The following letter, which has been addressed to us by a trustworthy correspondent this week shows a very different feeling upon the subject:— 'The following striking instance of the matter, in which the tender mercies of Romanists are shown towards those of their own communion who have been brought under a deep conviction of sin, to cry for mercy and pardon to the Lord Jesus Christ, will be read with both interest and horror.

"'A young man of the Roman Catholic religion, whose parents reside near Bellaghy in County Derry, went to live as a hired servant with a Protestant family not far from Ahoghill, where he came under the awakening influence now so widespread in that neighbourhood. Feeling himself unable to work, he resolved to return to his father's house for a few days, and accordingly left his master's residence for that purpose but, on arriving near home, he felt some alarm for his safety and sought lodgings for the night in the house of a Protestant family, where he was kindly received and put to bed by two Romanist servants.

"'These people soon noticed his changed conduct, and his earnestness in prayer to God. By their involvement, the news soon reached the young man's father that his son had become a Protestant revivalist. Great excitement ensued and, it being the Lord's Day, a large number of Roman Catholic neighbours soon assembled to bring back the straying child to his father's house.

"'The father received him not by falling on his neck and kissing him but by brutal violence of feet and hands in the hope, no doubt, that by these warning arguments he would soon be brought to his old way of thinking concerning religion. He was violently beaten even before entering the house. When inside, he was knocked down on the floor. Some were for hanging him, others were for knocking out his brains with a large mallet – and, during these inhuman proceedings, the young mother took an active part. All the unfortunate boy said, while subjected to this abuse was, 'You may kill my body, but you have no power over my soul.'

"'It was ultimately determined that the Priest should be sent for. But the Priest did not come on that day and on the day following the convert made his escape. He reached Portglenone in safety, in which place some Christian friends took care of him until he recovered sufficient strength to proceed to his master's house. The young man's name is O'Hara; his master's name is James Andrews; the owner of the house wherein he received lodgings for a night is Mr. McKennie of Ballymacpeake – his windows have since been broken.

"'Another remarkable occurrence took place in the same neighbourhood a few days ago. A young woman named Jackson, while proceeding from County Antrim to the home of a friend near Tamlaght O'Crilly, fell down under strong conviction upon the public road in a Roman Catholic district. She was left there without pity or assistance for the space of four hours. A mob assembled and discovered that she had a Psalm book. They destroyed a portion of the book, and then cut the figure of a cross upon the cover of the volume. The police were, at length, sent for but they seemed afraid to put their hands upon the suffering penitent, lest they should catch what is called by them 'the sleeping disease.'"

"Many other instances of a similar description might be mentioned, but this one is sufficient to show the feeling by which the more ignorant portion of the Roman Catholic community regard the gracious revival, with which we have been visited. This is not to be wondered at, for it is an undeniable fact that a larger number of the intelligent Roman Catholic people of Ulster have been influenced to embrace the Protestant religion within the last four months than during the preceding twenty years.

"In contrast with the previous painful exhibition of wickedness and bigotry, we feel pleasure in recording the declaration of a liberal and enlightened Roman Catholic Judge, namely Chief Pigott, as expressed at the Court held last week in County Down. His lordship, in reference to the religious movement, said that to an important extent it had extinguished religious and political hostility, and produced the most wholesome results upon the community at large. He described its operation in the most favourable terms, and concluded his observations with the expression of hope that it would extend over the whole country, and influence all ranks and conditions of society."

"The Banner of Ulster" Tuesday, 9th August 1859

Crossroads, Near Omagh

"On Sabbath evening, the 24th, a large district prayer meeting of the congregation was held in the open-air. A scene ensued; the most awful conviction that has been witnessed by any present in their day and generation. It was found necessary for some to remain during the night. One of the elders of the congregation stated that there were thirty cases of conviction, most of whom it is perfectly hoped may result in true conversion to the Saviour.

"The next evening, 25th July, a meeting was held in Crossroads Presbyterian Church and it turned out, under the Divine blessing, to be one of the most important ever held in that congregation, although established for seventy years. The number of people stricken down with heartfelt cries and appeals for mercy, through the length and breadth of a large house, was truly astonishing and awful. For whole hours neither singing nor prayer could be conducted. Every heart was subdued and brought to a depth of solemnity altogether unparalleled in the history of their lives. The meeting continued to near daylight. The number stricken and under conviction was between twenty five and thirty on that occasion."

Keady

"Steadily and savingly the work of God progresses. Never before have we realised the force of the Scriptural truth – 'Not by might, nor by power, but by My Spirit, saith the LORD.' For some time past the weekly prayer meeting in the neighbourhood has been attended by a large number, and a marked seriousness shown. The late visit of Mr. Moore of Ballymena had evidently produced a solemn thoughtfulness and anxiety, to see such as we never before witnessed reaching very many of the other religious denominations. Praise be to God we have now to record tokens of Almighty power, whose magnitude eternity alone can make known. Last Thursday was the usual day of humiliation before the quarterly Lord' Supper in the 1st Presbyterian congregation, Keady, when the Rev. Jackson Smyth of Armagh preached with great power and feeling on the 'great salvation'. The people heard as for eternity. When the services were over the people seemed loath to leave.

"A public meeting had been announced for six o'clock the same evening. Long before the appointed time, multitudes were thronging to the house of prayer and, at the hour of meeting, every available portion of the large church was filled – upwards of one thousand people within and around the doors. The service was opened with prayer and praise by Dr. Carson. The Rev. William Henderson of Armagh then addressed the people from the words, 'God our Saviour, and Lord Jesus Christ, Who is our hope', earnestly and eloquently dwelling on the practical religion of the great apostle, and urging everyone to know the Lord Jesus Christ as 'our hope'.

"The Rev. George Steen made a few remarks and references to his own experience of the great movement and led the audience in prayer and praise, when the Rev. Jackson Smyth delivered a thrilling address, riveting the attention of all present, dwelling with much feeling and beauty on the need of the Spirit's great work and on personal application of the blessed Jesus. As he spoke, we felt to be more and more 'of one mind'. Real faith was at work – an unseen Hand directed the arrows of conviction and, at once, several in the most heart piercing cries gave vent to their overburdened hearts, 'My sins, my sins!' 'My heart!' 'O, how hateful!' 'O, mercy, mercy, we felt as we never felt before.' As of truth we said, 'God is in this place – Spirit of the living God!'

"One such visit leads more into the knowledge of 'all truth' than the most laboured productions of the most accomplished minds. 'I thank Thee, O Father, Lord of Heaven and earth, because Thou hast hid these things from the wise and prudent, and hast revealed them unto babes. Even so, Father: for so it seemed good in Thy sight.'

Jehovah was in our midst and, as we heard the minister of the place express his solemn feelings, we were persuaded he then reaped a richer reward for twenty six years of ministerial life than if he had been presented with an earthly crown. The regular order of proceedings was discontinued and in groups here and there Christian friends, by reading the scriptures, and through prayer and praise ministered to sin-sick souls.

"Several others were removed to houses around, with salvation on their lips, and next morning we heard of many more who had passed a sleepless night still in agony, enduring all the bitterness of awakened, unforgiven sin. We cannot omit mentioning the case of one young man whose cries were loud and long continued. Having through the night found peace, on hearing in the morning of an acquaintance brought under conviction, he stole away to offer his sympathy and speak of Jesus. Surely is such amongst us; Jesus sees the travail of his soul and is satisfied. To sovereign grace be all the praise. As the wind comes and goes and no one can tell whence or where, so is everyone who is born of the Spirit. Let us cease from man, and in childlike weakness learn at last to hang on the Saviour, constant in prayer, giving to the God of Israel no rest 'til He arrives and makes Jerusalem a praise and a joy in the whole earth!"

"The Banner of Ulster" Thursday, 11th August 1859

The Present Religious Movement in the North

"We continue our truly gratifying report that, under the blessing of the Most High, He has chosen for the extension of His Kingdom in and beyond our borders. The number of praying and prayerful people continues to increase greatly. The revival may not, as at the beginning, be seen to grow by those who look to outward symptoms merely as evidence of conviction, but to others who derive their knowledge of it from intimate acquaintance with those whom the Spirit's power awakened – from Christian communion with them – and from following up the progress of their conversions, from the commencement by private visitation, union and prayer, it is truly and solemnly evident. They can testify with their lips and from their hearts that they have heard, and daily hear, hundreds pray who never prayed before. When the sanctuary, formerly half deserted upon the Sabbath, is now too small even during a more than usual beautiful summer, even on the evening after a day's toil, it is also too small to accommodate the crowds who pass its doors to learn of the Saviour's undying love, surely it can be said that the work which is going forward is indeed of God. When among the working classes, from the smooth brow to the furrowed cheek and hairy locks, the glad tidings of great joy is the theme of earnest conversation in the workshop and in the quiet home – even on the public pathway – so different from the frivolous and often profane interchange of thought that not long since prevailed, it cannot be doubted that a great and blessed change is being wrought in the heart of the community and that by a Power Who works by means that we know not of.

"Were we at liberty to record the particulars of a case in which, by the unquestionable influence of the Holy Spirit operating upon the heart and understanding, the careless and unconcerned have been stirred up to a sense of their danger – the cold and sneering roused to think of their lost state by nature – and the reckless and unrestrained are entirely turned from the errors of their past lives – we could, by names, dates, and localities furnish such statistics of the progress of the revival movement as must convince the most sceptical of its reality and extent.

"The regular and habitual holding of prayer meetings in the private homes of both the humbler and middle classes in the evenings, after the labour has finished, has now become so common as to excite little remark. In passing along some of the streets the voice of prayer and praise may frequently be heard at such times from several houses at once. Two evenings since, in a northern suburb of the town where the clusters of houses are detached, our cars were greeted at a distance with the harmonious swellings of sounds of a well known hymn, attended by some fifty voices. Some hundreds of yards away rose the noisy concord of an amateur brass band rehearsing for a forthcoming fete. The latter ceased as the melody of the hymn reached the ears of the performers and to their credit, be it spoken, they disturbed it no more."

Queen's Island

"Revival prayer meetings are kept up on the central lawn of the beautiful grounds of public recreation and of a busy industry. They are informally held during the hour allowed for the numerous workmen in Mr. Harland's extensive ship building and iron works to have dinner. Many of the workers dine at the works and, after hastily eating the meal, cheerfully and earnestly join in the religious worship conducted in their vicinity by a Christian gentleman who attends there for that purpose. It is known that these services have been attended with happy results."

Lambeg

"Last evening a revival prayer meeting was held at the extensive bleach works of Messrs. Richardson, Lambeg. It was attended not only by a large number of the workers employed there, but also by many of those engaged in the mill of Messrs. Barber and Sons at Hilden, as well as by workers connected with the different other manufacturers in the neighbourhood. Shortly after seven o'clock the people began to assemble in great numbers to hear an interesting address given by a Belfast gentleman. When they were all assembled together there could not have been fewer than twelve hundred present. The whole immense multitude listened with intense anxiety to the words of exhortation and instruction addressed to them, and many of them seemed deeply affected. Two people were stricken down under conviction of sin and removed from the place. The impression made on the audience was very marked, and the meeting altogether was one of the most interesting which had been held for a length of time, within the same distance of Belfast."

Newtownards

"The gracious work of the Spirit is steadily advancing here. In a town of more than ten thousand inhabitants it may be expected that the movement, even at its present rapid rate of advancement, will be a considerable time in effecting a thorough change, but already the change is so great that it has become one of the ordinary topics of conversation. The Sabbath, which had often been kept in many houses as a day of special feasting and revelry, is now so strictly observed that the stillness of the streets is seldom broken except by the crowds who flock to several churches. A few drunkards may still be seen at rare intervals staggering on the footpath, but drunkenness is so far abated that it may be said to be almost gone. Some weeks ago a bargain could scarcely be made on the market day without drink and the payment of wages was, in very many cases, immediately followed by a visit to the public house. But now the rule is exactly reversed. Districts of the town that on Saturday evenings used to be so turbulent the very police were timid in following people who had taken refuge there, are now perfectly quiet and peaceful.

"In one district of this kind the weavers now spend a part of each Saturday evening fitting up, with their 'seat boards', an apartment in the neighbourhood in which a prayer meeting is held on Sabbath afternoon. Instead of the noisy sounds with which in such localities the week was often closed, the first thing that frequently catches the ear now is the singing of hymns with grave sweet melody in the houses of the stricken. It is indeed a common thing to find the people affected surrounded by a band whose hearts the Lord has touched acting the part of the good Samaritan, in pouring oil on the spiritual wounds, and it is often with no small surprise that a visitor recognises, in the very leader of the band, a person whose mouth was lately full of 'cursing and bitterness'.

"It is needless to state that the effects of the movement are not confined to any one class or society. The physical accompaniments may not be equally found in all classes, but it would perhaps be difficult to state which has received the greatest spiritual benefit. There is plainly a Power at work here Who is rapidly changing the character of the whole social fabric, though in some parts the changes may be wrought, as in the building of the temple, without the sound of either hammer or axe. It may also be remarked that persons of all religious denominations of the town have been brought under the Spirit's power and it hardly requires to be added that, whatever they were, they invariably adopt Paul's determination to know nothing but Jesus Christ and Him crucified. The sentiments expressed by a convert from an utterly false religion are often as purely evangelical as those of one who had been taught the truth from childhood. Besides the ordinary services in the various churches during the week, the meeting for united prayer in the 1ˢᵗ Presbyterian Church is still attended with such unabated interest the large building is always filled to overflowing."

Donaghadee

"For the last fortnight the good work has proceeded steadily here. In the early part of last week there were a great many prostrations, but for the last few days they have been considerably decreased. On Tuesday evening a very large open-air prayer meeting was held with about two thousand people present. The meeting was addressed by several gentlemen. A number of people had to be assisted to their homes, crying out under the weight of their sins and are now rejoicing in the mercy and love of their Redeemer; but, as is the universal experience, these extraordinary cases give but a very imperfect idea of the number of those who are seriously impressed about their souls' welfare and who are led to enquire, 'What must I do to be saved?' A great change, evident to all, has taken place in the whole face of society.

"Our town has a long and unenviable notoriety for drunkenness, but now a drunken man is rarely to be seen. The mouth of the profane swearer is also stopped – Sunday, made the most unholy day of all the seven, is now observed as a Sabbath – and many crowd the houses of worship who were never known to cross their threshold before. Two years ago open-air preaching attempted by various ministers of the assembly had to be abandoned for want of congregations; now anyone who wishes to hold a prayer meeting or preach on the street can, on any evening, have an audience of one thousand to one thousand five hundred people.

"Is this state of things like the devil's work, as has been unjustifiably asserted by clergymen? Does Satan stir up the people to erect a family altar, to read the Bible, to attend prayer meetings, to crowd the House of God? Does he induce the drunkard to forsake his cups, the profane swearer his cursing, and the Sabbath-breaker to abide in the Lord's tent on that holy day? Yet these things have taken place and, it is strange to say, there are clergymen here who refuse to endorse the movement and assert, even publicly, that these prostrations are all caused by overcrowded, overheated houses, acting on excitable, nervous temperaments. Not withstanding all this opposition, the friends of the movement have kept up prayer meetings, both in the open-air and in the churches, and have secured the services of various clergymen from a distance who have had, in every instance, such large and attentive audiences as were never convened in this town before.

"Yesterday evening, the 10th, the Rev. Messrs. Thompson of Crossgar and Cather of Newtownards addressed a meeting of fifteen hundred people on the street. Dr. Begg from Edinburgh preached in Mr. McCauley's church yesterday and who, for some time has been investigating the matter in the North of Ireland, gave his weighty evidence in favour of the genuineness of the movement. An incident occurred on Sabbath evening last in a neighbouring church which was too good to be lost. The 'powers that be' in that congregation are also unfavourable to the movement, and two young men were brought from Belfast to demonstrate that the revivals were merely a temporary excitement. Well, one of these young 'Goliaths', when addressing a prayer meeting on the night in question, stated boldly that all these bodily prostrations were nervous affections brought on by exciting speeches and asserted that he could, by the power of his language, so excite them and string their nerves to such attention that he could prostrate every man, woman and child before him! A countryman rose up and, stretching his arms, addressed the gentleman:– 'You have said you can by your own words, prostrate everyone in the house. Now, here am I, try your hand on me. You can't prostrate me.' The minister came and desiring him to sit down and be quiet, reminded him that it was a prayer meeting. 'No,' said he, 'I will not sit down. He says he can prostrate all in the house: but I believe nothing but the power of the Lord Jesus can prostrate anyone. Let him go on and try his hand on me.' It was, however, considered better not to try the experiment."

Monaghan

"All around the central town – in places where the Protestant population are much in the minority – the glorious work of the revival movement is awakening many. A few evenings ago, in a locality about three miles from Monaghan, a revival prayer meeting was held in a large barn and no fewer than ten people were stricken down during the religious worship. At another meeting five miles from the town, a still greater manifestation of the Spirit's presence and power took place. The number of outward manifestations of conviction accounted to upwards of thirty.

"In the same neighbourhood more than three hundred people are known to have come under the influence of the awakening Spirit. In fact almost every second person in the district is in this hopeful state. The Rev. Mr. Reid of Banchory addressed a meeting in the 2nd Presbyterian congregation of Monaghan on Thursday evening and, on the following evening, one in the 1st congregation. At the last meeting two people were stricken down. Young men meet together every evening for prayer – generally converts – and the results of those meetings are already visible in the changed conduct of the people they address."

Castlederg, County Tyrone

"I am glad to inform you that the great and glorious work of the Lord in this place, as noticed by me lately, is greatly on the increase. On 24th July three young men from Londonderry, Messrs. Dickson, Donnolly and McGowan, together with the Reverends Crawford, Armstrong, Love and Ralston who are Presbyterian ministers and the Rev. Mr. Doonan, a Wesleyan minister in the place, addressed over four thousand people in the open-air in Dr. Motherwell's field at Castlederg. Two young converts also addressed the meeting – one a young man from the town of Castlederg who thanked God that he had heard the young men from Londonderry. Many in the county told me how the Lord made them instrumental in their conversion. The Lord has significantly honoured their labours among us.

"A much larger meeting was addressed on 31st July in the same place by the deputation from Londonderry and the above ministers. On 7th August there were about five thousand in attendance when the deputation from Londonderry, the Presbyterian ministers, and the Rev. Mr. Whittiger, a Wesleyan minister, took part in the services. At all these times there were several cases of conviction and conversion, both in the field and at the prayer meetings in the different places of worship, and also after leaving the field at eight o'clock. It is delightful to see whole families rejoicing in the Lord as Saviour at our fellowship meetings and, when they meet in the house of the Lord for worship, they rejoice 'and tell to all around what a Saviour they have found.'

"The great success of the revivals in this place has caused the prince of darkness to stir up the minds of Roman Catholics against us. On Friday last, the 5th, it being the Fair Day in the town, while the Rev. W. Doonan, a Wesleyan minister, was holding his usual open-air service in the street, which in no way interfered with the public thoroughfare, a large disorderly mob (whom I believe were brought from a distance on purpose) commenced to whistle and shout and throw stones. One of the stones passing by the preacher's head struck a girl on the bonnet. They continued in this manner until he finished, when they followed him to his lodgings yelling and shouting in a most frightful way and they assembled around his lodgings for some time in this way. As the minister was protected by the Constabulary and some of the respectable inhabitants of the town and county, they fortunately did him no harm. I hope in the carrying out of the great commission of our Divine Master to preach the gospel to every creature, whether they will hear or whether they will refrain, that the implementation will so honour the spirit of our laws as will prevent any occurrence of a like nature again, and cause us to worship the Lord according to our conscience."

"The Ballymena Observer" Saturday, 13th August 1859

"On Monday a new and very extraordinary case of contrite conviction occurred, in the person of an aged man who, up to that day, was well known as one of the most reckless characters in Ballymena. He professed to be a Unitarian, but his connection with that or any other communion was only nominal. He was notorious as a mocker of the revivalists, and said that the half of them were imposters and the other half were stark mad. While at his work, before the breakfast hour on Monday morning, he was cursing and swearing at them most terribly.

"Before noon, this hardened man was prostrate, conscience-smitten and repenting. He had been suddenly 'stricken' while at breakfast in his own house! Great fear had come upon him and, while in mental agony and shivering in every muscle of his body, he implored some godly neighbours to sing Psalms beside him. An evangelical minister was sent for. He visited the sufferer, prayed with him and encouraged him to look to Jesus as the only means of salvation. The man was submissive in spirit and expressed his entire conviction that, out of Christ, there was no hope for him.

"While in this state of mind he was also visited by a man in whose hearing he had blasphemed God, and cursed the revivalists only a few hours before. The humble sinner now caught him by the hand and burst into tears. 'Ah!' said he, 'I used to think that the revivalists were acting, but now I know that God's hand is in the work.' Then, pressing his hands over the region of his heart, he exclaimed, 'Oh, there is no deviousness here!' We know a gentleman who had a few minutes conversation with the awakened man the following day. He had resumed his ordinary labour, but felt unusually weak. He did not profess to have found peace with God, but his manner was solemn. He had begun to think, and he expressed a hope that the awful visitation had been one of mercy, and that it would be an abiding influence upon his heart."

"The Banner of Ulster" Saturday, 13th August 1859

Conlig

"The work of religious revival seems to be making amazing progress in County Down, especially within the boundaries of Ards, Castlereagh and Dufferin. I have been through this part of the country lately and can bear testimony to the character and importance of the movement. The effects are clear. That which makes men honest, sober, humble, prayerful and holy must be good. Houses of worship are now crammed – congregations are devout and solemnised beyond all precedent. Family altars are being erected or repaired throughout the land. The preaching of the Presbyterian ministers is exceedingly eloquent and impressive, and the fruits of righteousness, which are by Jesus Christ, to the praise and glory of God, gladden the Christian's heart wherever in this fine county he turns his eyes.

"I shall give your readers one fact which is conclusive in my mind as the character of this revival. Having resided with my family for some time at Bangor, I worshipped last Sabbath in the Presbyterian Church of Conlig. It was the communion Sabbath – a day that will be long remembered by the people of that place. I was informed after the service that the number of communicants was doubled – that is, as many more sat down at the table of the Saviour's love as had ever done before. Mr. Hanson, the minister of the place, was assisted by his brother, the Rev. David Hanson of Faughan. There was no attempt made to excite the people, indeed there seemed, on the part of both ministers, a desire to restrain rather than encourage manifestation of feeling; and yet the tears that trickled down the cheeks of women, children and old men, throughout the whole service, testified to the deep emotion that swelled and surged in every breast.

"The sermon of the morning was eloquent and Scriptural, and in it the minister dwelt on the promises of the New Covenant and the love of Jesus to sinners. I could not but think of the refreshing shower of grace that accompanied Livingstone's preaching at Shotts, or the more abundant descent of the Spirit which marked the Apostles era. Happy are the people who are in such a case; yea, happy are the people whose God is the Lord!"

Rathfriland

"Cases of prostration are not now so numerous, but anxious enquirers may be found in almost every house. Many who were impressed at the beginning of the movement are now rejoicing in Christ or busily engaged in evangelizing around the neighbourhood. The hunger and thirst for the Word of life almost exceeds belief. At a moment's notice a congregation can be had in any quarter and none more eager than a street which was, a few months ago, the disgrace of the town. People are seen along the streets or country roads sitting in the sun and reading the Bible or religious tracts. As long as the speakers can continue to address them so long will the thirsty multitudes continue to listen and this in spite of the weather, even when it is unfavourable which is seldom.

"Local prayer meetings have multiplied beyond reckoning. In one evening there may be a hundred such meetings in the town and neighbourhood, with results that nothing but eternity will declare. Meanwhile, families notoriously ungodly and unruly – disturbers of the peace – have become homes of prayer, with the inmates sitting clothed and in their right mind at the feet of Jesus. The streets resound with the singing of Psalms, a marked soberness characterises the weekly markets and a general widespread deepening sense of Divine things is observed by all. Some poor families have lost considerably by being some days off work during their weakness, yet the visitor scarcely ever hears a murmur, even from persons who formerly could be got to speak of nothing but their poverty. These, and many others, are the cheering and blessed fruits of the movement amongst us and, while love to Jesus is the burden on every voice and prayer by the occupation of every spare moment, we cannot but hope the Lord is adding to the Church daily such as shall be saved. The revival movement goes on in the neighbouring congregations in Brockville, Annaghlone, Glasscar, Ryans, Closkelt, Ballyroney, Drumlee, Castlewellan and Clonduff; they have all experienced the visitation in some degree. The great majority of the cases of conviction are most hopeful – in some instances they are mysterious. The subjects of the work are affected differently and with different results."

Drumnakeen

"The Rev. W. Cooke sends us the following report from his own congregation:– 'I rejoice to be able to state that God is doing great things in my congregation here. Returning from the meeting of our assembly I found that the Spirit of God had been before me. Salvation had come to one house and heart. Since then the Holy Spirit has been working mightily among us. Here He distils like the gentle dew upon the soul, there He brings very low to the ground until the soul cries with an exceedingly bitter cry:– 'Lord Jesus, take away my sins!' I have been compelled to give over a service to the public congregation for the sighs and sobs and bitter cries of sin-burnt souls, and from speaking and proclaiming the gospel I love, with tears of joy, and turn to the sweet and holy and reviving service of praise and song.

"'To give an incident or two amongst many – on Sabbath last I was called to visit a sin-sick soul after a divine service. I went in and engaged in the sweet work of pointing that soul to the Saviour Whom he sought. I addressed a few solemn words to the other members of the family and, before I left, a second member of the household was bathed in tears. I came home and retired to rest but, in half an hour, three messengers were seeking me. I went back to the same house I had left a short time ago, where two souls were now seeking mercy. I began to speak and another member of the family seemed deeply attentive. I again related the story of the Saviour's love and, after singing and a prayer, I arose and left but before I was very far from that house I heard, slightly after midnight, the tramp of footsteps nearer and nearer. I turned round. There was a messenger from the same house that a third was crying out for pardon of sins, and I was constrained to return. And what a house! – a humble cottage, but more honoured than a palace. The King of kings is there! 'How dreadful this house!' There were three sisters, two of them were rejoicing in the mercy of God in Christ Jesus when last I saw them; the third was seeking peace through the blood of the Saviour – and resolved to continue seeking until she would find it.

"'Three young men, brothers in another family of high standing amongst us, have been brought to Jesus. A maidservant in the same house has been added to the Lord. Daily and nightly now you hear songs of praise where you could have heard none before – prayer where none prayed before – God's Word in the hands of both old and young where the novel or the newspaper was found before. The churches are literally crammed to the door – aisles and all – whether on the Sabbath or on a weekday. Our prayer meetings, which are held in houses of the members of the congregation on Monday, Tuesday, Wednesday, and Thursday evenings are congregations of three, four, five, six and seven hundred persons of all denominations. What God hath wrought! Two weeks ago we had the privilege of hearing addresses from two laymen, Messrs. Fulton and Hogg from Ahoghill – first fruits of the revival – and much good was the result.

"'I had been holding my daily prayer meetings before their coming and much awakening had taken place and much earnestness had been shown, and wherever I went I was privileged to find crowds already gathered, not struggling in now and again, but waiting with open Bibles and solemn expectation upon the service of God. The meetings addressed by these servants of God and held in the open-air – for the church could not have admitted much beyond half of the people – ushered in the second phase of the work of His manifestations.

"'One case indeed occurred previously in the solemn silence of midnight, but more have happened since and they take place, not so much at our meetings as after they are over – when the people are on their way home – when they are in their houses. Many also have undergone – enjoyed rather – the work of regeneration without any physical prostration, and are now sitting at every opportunity in the House of God and in the prayer meeting, rejoicing in their Lord. I am called often to visit another seeking one and cannot give you any further account just now.'"

The Rev. Mr. Somerville on the Revival in Ireland

"The Rev. Mr. Somerville of Anderston's Free Church, who paid a visit to the North of Ireland last week, was present at the daily prayer meeting in the religious institution rooms, Glasgow, on Monday and gave a brief account of what he had seen. His impression was that a great and glorious work was going on in the North of Ireland. On going into a bookseller's shop in Coleraine, the shopkeeper told him that she seldom sold any novels now, but that she sold a great number of religious books. On the previous Saturday the shopkeeper said she had sold religious books to the country people round about Coleraine to the extent of seven or eight pounds.

"Afterwards he visited a number of the persons on whom a change had been wrought, in company with Mr. Horner who was very kind and who promised to come over again from Glasgow soon. He had been told that it was scarcely possible to step into a draper's or grocer's shop in Coleraine without finding one or more of the young men seriously impressed, and he found this to be true. There was now a prayer meeting of young men every evening at which there was an average attendance of about fifty.   One of the ministers of Coleraine told him that he had met the Chief Constable of Coleraine and he told him that, whereas in former years fifty convictions before the magistrate generally took place after the 12th July, there was this year only four. The Superintendent of Excise in the same district mentioned that, during the two months of June and July, only one-tenth of the revenue came in from spirits that was received in any previous two months he had been in charge. Near Coleraine he had heard of a prayer meeting which continued two and half days without intermission.   One of the ministers of Coleraine told him that twelve prayer meetings have existed in this congregation for twelve years and, about a year ago when the good news came from America, these meetings were greatly quickened and enlarged."

"The Banner of Ulster" Tuesday, 16th August 1859

Malin

"It is now six weeks since the revival commenced here and never, in any place I have visited, have I seen such a great change. People who have not attended their house of prayer for a period of twenty five years have been brought to the knowledge of their unrighteousness and are now regular attenders. Family prayer has been established where it never was. Drunkards, blasphemers and suchlike have turned from the evil tendency of their ways and seek the truth, as it is in Jesus, with sincerity. Prayer meetings are held every morning at eight o'clock in the Rev. John Canning's. On Tuesdays and Fridays meetings are held at four different places at seven o'clock and on Wednesdays at the meeting house. Last Wednesday the congregation was addressed by the Rev. Dr. Kirkpatrick, the Rev. A. Pinkerton and the Rev. John Canning. A convert from Londonderry has addressed the congregation several times, and I hope was the means of bringing many to the knowledge of their sins."

Dunmull Hill

"On Sabbath last an immense meeting was held for religious purposes on Dunmull Hill about three miles from Bushmills. The number who assembled upon that occasion could not have been fewer than seven thousand. The meeting was addressed by two lay Christian converts from Connor and afterwards by Mr. Brownlow North. The latter gentleman was obliged to speak a second time because of the immense assembly who were present, many of whom remained for a long period after the meeting had been expected to terminate, exhibiting a great anxiety to hear what fell from the lips of the eloquent speaker. All the addresses were of the most edifying description – particularly that of Mr. North. While they were being delivered a large number of people were stricken down under conviction of sin, and among the remainder, from the beginning to the end, a deep solemnity pervaded the meeting. The Rev. J. Simpson of Portrush also took part in the religious services."

Bailieborough

"I have been thinking that you might wish to get some account of the revival movement in this neighbourhood. Two young men from Rathfriland have been up here holding meetings for the last few days. They held a field meeting on the evening of the 9th. The Rev. Mr. White opened the service with singing and prayer and then introduced Mr. Herron, a tall, dark complexioned young man, apparently much fatigued. You would think by looking at him that his physical energies were overtaxed. Mr. Herron was, above all things, earnest. He pictured the torments of the damned, contrasted them with the happiness of the just, spoke of the work of true religion as progressing in the neighbourhood of Rathfriland and called on his hearers vehemently to choose whom they would serve. He spoke for about three-quarters of an hour and, when he left the platform, Mr. Patterson came forward, gave but a few verses of a Psalm and commenced to make a few remarks before they would engage in singing. This was the turning point.

"He called upon them not to engage in singing God's praise if they were not firmly resolved to praise Him with their whole hearts as well as with their lips, and asked them how long would they reject the mercy which was offered. These remarks caused much crying among the female portion of the audience, and the verses of the Psalm were hardly commenced when I heard a few sharp cries beside me and, looking around, I saw a young woman in the act of falling from her seat. She was immediately surrounded by her friends and her head placed in the lap of her mother. Mr. Patterson called them to keep quiet and keep their places, that it was nothing unusual – or why should it be? – to see a poor sinner afraid of Hell and crying to the Lord for mercy. The Psalm was again taken up but before one verse had been sung, one, two, three, more in the same neighbourhood of the meeting had fallen over helpless. It was now very hard to restrain the people from rushing to that part of the congregation. Numbers were pushing forward to have their curiosity satisfied. But for this crisis the speaker seemed prepared. He turned to the opposite side and by addressing them there arrested the tide.

"There was surely nothing irrational about the conduct of the fallen. Their almost continual cry was, 'O, Saviour, pardon, pardon!' or language to that effect. I asked those around them why they did not remove them out of the crowd where the atmosphere would not have been so oppressive and was answered by, I think, that they were very well and would soon be whole in Jesus Christ. I am told that, amongst the number, there were one or two young men who had to be carried down the field to the open space, but I did not see them. The meeting broke up about nine o'clock but many remained in the field 'til after ten o'clock – some praying for mercy and others praising God.

"There was surely a great union of sects, if I may so speak; the Rev. William Gumbley of the Church of England, the Rev. Patrick White, Presbyterian, and a Wesleyan minister whose name I cannot tell, were all engaged together in prayer. There was no madness, and no one listening to those prayers and seeing those tears streaming down the cheeks of many would say it was.

"The Banner of Ulster" Thursday, 18th August 1859

"The present week has been one of the most remarkable seasons of spiritual awakening that has passed in this city since the tidal wave of religious revival began among us. We do not speak of it merely as the work of a great revival meeting but as one in which many souls have been brought to Jesus by humble activity in the by-lanes and the formerly neglected outskirts of our great and bustling city.

"Strange it is that among a population so thoroughly devoted to business, and that of the most trying nature, as the people of Belfast are, the revival work should have found a centre here from which the movement has radiated in a degree and with a power altogether remarkable. We have become a people to be regarded – to be looked upon as especially favoured – and as a section of the Christian Church to be held up an example to our neighbouring brethren, and even in country districts.

"We have now, however, to speak of a meeting which has been witnessed by thousands and, in the proceedings of which, many have taken part.

Second Great Meeting for United Prayer

"In a record of the immense union prayer meeting in connection with the revival movement held in the Royal Botanic Gardens, Belfast, held on the 20th June, we described it as one of the greatest crowds for a religious purpose ever held in the United Kingdom. We have now to inform you of another meeting for united prayer held in the same place on Tuesday, which is almost equal to the former in point of numbers and in its results quite as important. The total number of the immense multitude who had been brought together, not only from this town but from various other places along the different lines of railway, fluctuated from time to time but we do not overestimate it when we state that we saw at one time at least twenty thousand people in the gardens.

"The attendance would have been considerably larger than this had it not been that the morning, up to the forenoon, was exceedingly cloudy and that it rained smartly at times. This deterred people from proceeding to the gardens. Even those who had made arrangements for taking their families with them were encouraged to stay at home by the state of the clouds. As the time approached however the day cleared up and, although there was little sunshine, the rest of the day was fair and pleasant while the meeting lasted. Immediately afterwards the sky suddenly darkened as if a thunderstorm was impending, and rain fell in torrents.

"The meeting had been announced for only a very short time – much shorter than the previous one. Subsequently many who would have attended knew nothing of it.

"The Belfast Young Men's Christian Association", who organised this great meeting, is not widely known as it should be. This was another reason why the 'monster meeting' was not larger than it was. Still, we saw upon the grounds – everything considered – ten country people for everyone that would have been expected. From remote portions of Antrim – from far away districts in Down – from portions of Armagh, where the scythe is busy in the harvest field – from Tyrone, where Presbyterians are staunch but few and far between – we saw numerous groups in the garden all apparently earnest in the cause which had brought them together. These consisted, for the most part, of young people respectable in dress and manner – evidently of the better class of tenant farmers and families, and most of them accompanied by fathers, brothers or husbands. A better, a fairer or more honest specimen of the descendents of the Scottish settlers in Ulster – of the men who bore Bible in the right hand – has never before been presented upon a field in Ulster or upon an occasion when it could be seen to so much advantage.

"A working day in the industrious city of Belfast, nearly in the middle of the week, is a strange time for the holding of a great meeting. Nevertheless, had there been no influx of visitors from the country present, the crowd of Tuesday would have been great. We are grateful that a number of large employers in Belfast closed their works for the occasion in order to allow their workers an opportunity of being present at the meeting.

"The meeting was announced for twelve o'clock, and twenty thousand tickets of admission had previously been issued. It was found that even this immense number would not be sufficient to meet the demands upon the occasion. A public announcement was made by posters that entrance to the gardens could be obtained by respectable people without any special ticket. We should therefore say that, in addition to those holding tickets, half as many again visited the grounds during the four hours occupied by the meeting and, where present, at either of the general services, or at those which were held in detached portions of the grounds.

"There were numbers of people from Scotland present – ministers and laymen of various congregations from east to west and from north to south of the land of Knox. Some of these took part in the devotional services and all expressed themselves astonished and delighted in a work which having commenced in a portion of the Christian field that was least to have been expected, is now sowing its seeds in the land producing, we trust, good fruit.

"The beautiful grounds of the Royal Botanic Gardens are, at this season, in full abundance of foliage – much more so than in the leafy month of June when the former meeting was held. They therefore afforded opportunity for a division of Christian labour. Newest groups assembled in suitable spots here and there over the wide expanse of the grounds, for the purpose of praise and prayer while the services were being conducted in the central part of the gardens in front of the permanent pavilion. Some of these were presided over by ministers eager in the work of revival – others by converts, and the latter were both the most numerous and the most interesting.

"We shall not individualise the groups who assembled for praise and for prayer in various portions of the grounds, but rather refer to them by numbers.

"Group number six was conducted in a most proper way. A young girl about eighteen years of age was stricken down during the services. She had, it appears, been under a deep conviction of sin for a long time. One or two Christian brethren visited her from time to time and prayed with her and for her. At length she was able to express her joy at finding peace in Jesus. We must mention, however, that not long after this she was deprived of speech. The muscles of her jaws became stiff and her tongue paralysed.

"A Christian friend was called upon to visit her and did so. He said, 'I fear that the Lord has thus visited you for some sin you have habitually committed against Him with your tongue. If, however, you feel conviction of that sin and are willing to repent of it and to glorify Him in body and in soul, we will pray for you.' The stricken female signified by gesture her willingness that this should be done. Her wish was complied with and, after the song of praise had been raised, 'I am not ashamed to own my Lord' and, while prayer was being offered up, her tongue was loosed – she sang, she prayed and gave thanks to God, and was afterwards taken to her home rejoicing in the Name of the Lord in Whom she had found peace.

"In the centre of another group the most remarkable of all was a poor chimney-sweeper – a stalwart youth – evidently attracted to the gardens by no motive but mere curiosity. He listened with solemn attention to the prayer and to all the rest of the proceedings and, while they were going on he was so much affected that he wept like a child and openly confessed himself a sinner. He besought a Christian leader near him to engage in prayer on his behalf. This request was once acceded to. The 53rd chapter of Isaiah was read and expounded, and this riveted the attention of all who were around. It is hoped that several instances of conversion have resulted from this little meeting.

"Another group was presided over by the Rev. Thomas Toye who offered up a most impressive prayer and then addressed his audience from a portion of the Word of God. During the time that he was thus engaged one of the most interesting instances of the day took place – mainly, the arrival in the grounds of the converts of his congregation, male and female, a considerable number who approached in procession, in a solemn manner and singing songs of praise to the Most High. After engaging in the services of the day they left the garden in the same manner, attracting the marked attention of all who were present. They proceeded in the same manner down the Botanic Road, passed the Linen Hall, and so to Great George's Street Church.

"A very interesting circumstance occurred at the close of Rev. Toye's address. He asked those who were anxious about preparing to meet God in peace, to kneel down in instant prayer after the example of Christ in the garden. Almost every person responded to the call. The group numbered nearly nine hundred people.

"A further group of prayerful people was formed, at first by six young converts averaging from eight to eleven years of age. After the singing of a portion of a Psalm, one of them offered up the most original and impressive prayer we ever heard. When he had finished, the prayer was resumed by a convert still younger whose sentiments of love struck everyone around. He prayed not only for the Children of God in Belfast, but for those around him who had not already found peace in Jesus, and afterwards for the unconverted all throughout the world. The effect of this prayer upon the bystanders was very marked. At its conclusion an eminent Christian from Scotland remarked to a friend, 'Oh, Sir! Did you ever listen to pleading at the Throne of Grace such as these? I never before heard anything like them, and they shall never pass from my memory.'

"With one other group we shall conclude our description of this portion of the day's proceedings. Its principle feature was a poor little boy – a messenger in town. After a Psalm had been sung, he knelt down in prayer and uttered desires at once beautiful in sentiment and in language. During this time a strong healthy young woman was stricken down and gave vent to her feelings with piercing cries. Such was her mental agony for some time that the physical powers of four muscular men scarcely sufficed to keep her in a respectable position. She afterwards recovered however and we have reason to hope that the poor young woman is in a hopeful state both physically and spiritually.

"We give below an outline of the proceedings from the platform. The weather, fortunately, did not at any time interrupt the proceedings, gloomy and threatening as the sky looked. No sooner, however, had the services closed that the rain commenced to pour down.

"We were glad to observe that most of the visitors from the country had left the grounds in sufficient time before this occurred, to meet the railway trains in which they had secured return tickets.

"The Rev. Robert Knox discharged the duties of President of the meeting. Shortly after midday the President came to the front of the platform and expressed a hope that in order for everyone in that large audience to hear, perfect silence would be maintained during prayer and exhortation. He then called on the meeting to join in singing the 100th Psalm and, at its conclusion, the Rev. Knox offered up a prayer. He then requested that people should remain, if possible, in one place for if order were not maintained it would be impossible that they would hear what his brethren had to say.

"They should remember that God was in their midst for He had said that where two or three were gathered together in His Name there would He be. God was watching their proceedings that day and he asked them to join in the spirit of expectation for the power of His Holy Spirit. God had said, 'Open your mouth wide and I will fill it.' He would graciously bless those who were deserving, who were willing and who were expecting a blessing from Him. If they came there for the purpose of frequently calling upon God for His mercy – if they came there to wait upon Him – if they came there in a true spirit expecting His blessing, he (the President) believed in his soul that not one of them would leave the garden without a blessing.

"If any of them went away without the Spirit of God in their hearts it was because they did not seek the mercy of their Heavenly Father. Let them unite with one heart and with one mind to seek the blessing of God and it would not be withheld from them. He (the President) rejoiced at the present meeting. He thanked God for it, and he trusted and believed in his conscience that they would not meet in vain, but that the Lord would meet with them and bless.

"The Rev. William Johnston then came forward and read the 53rd chapter of Isaiah. The Rev. Hugh Hanna called the meeting to sing the 98th Psalm, 'Oh sing a new song to the Lord'. Afterwards the Rev. Gentleman offered up prayer. At its conclusion, he proceeded to remark that from the days of Isaiah to the present time the people did not truly know the Spirit of their Divine Master. To be sure many made a profession of a belief in God's holy grace, but had these people truly considered the awful responsibility under which they rested? I dare say there were hundreds who, up to the last three weeks, had not considered the blessings which flowed from the Word of God nor knew what it was to consider, what it was to call upon God with earnest prayer for an extension of His powers of saving grace.

"How many among them had withheld from God the testimony of their hearts? How many among them had left His claims on their affection and love unconsidered? How many had disregarded the responsibility unto which their own souls rested? Were they prepared to leave their immortal souls uncared for 'til they were called upon to appear before the Great Judgement bar of Heaven? Oh! What a curse would fall if they did not see the errors of their worldly conduct 'til the awful day of condemnation! He appealed to them, as sinners, not to let the testimony of that day be registered against them, but to prepare themselves for meeting their Heavenly Father at the Last Day. Above all, let them remember what earthly gain would recompense them for the loss of their own souls."

Magherally

"On Sabbath the 14ᵗʰ, the annual sermon to the Sabbath School children in this Parish and neighbourhood was preached by the Rev. James Thompson from Psalm 71:17:— 'O God, Thou hast taught me from my youth.' The sermon was well adapted to the youthful part of the congregation. There were five Sabbath Schools present – Mullafernaghan, Magherally, Chinauley, Ballydown and Ballyroney – above five hundred children. Every school was examined separately on the sermon which was preached and on other doctrines of the Bible. The answering was exceedingly good – all questions were distinctly answered. There could not be less than twelve hundred people present. Hundreds had to stand outside the doors and windows. There was more than usual solemnity over the face of the audience and we have no doubt that many were rejoicing in God, through our Lord Jesus Christ.

"The great work of revival is still going on in this Parish and other districts around it. The rector of the Parish and the curate go hand in hand with the Rev. Mr. Thomas in holding prayer meetings. Some have been stricken down under deep conviction of sin, and many more in their own homes have had their hearts opened, seeking the Lord by prayer and have found Him. The good work is spreading rapidly in the town of Banbridge, and the ministers in that town are labouring night and day in directing the convicted ones to Jesus. One girl, lately affected and crying for mercy when brought home, threw her arms about her mother's neck and kissed her, and cried out, 'O mother, will you not come with me to Jesus?'"

Bailieborough

"We are truly gratified to state that the work of the Lord – the great awakening – has now reached the southern part of Ulster and manifested itself in County Cavan, at Bailieborough, with a Power previously we might almost say unprecedented in any place. On Monday evening a meeting was held in the Presbyterian Church of 1st Bailieborough. It was opened by the Rev. Patrick White and afterwards addressed by Messrs. Herron and Patterson from the North. This large place of worship was completely filled. An open-air meeting was held on Tuesday morning, and a large number assembled. Mr. White again opened the meeting and was followed by two youthful ambassadors for Christ, who proclaimed the truth, as it is in Jesus, with a fervency and impressiveness that made tears of sorrow and contrition roll down many a furrowed cheek.

"At six o'clock in the evening the same gentlemen held a meeting at Bailieborough in the open-air – the congregation numbered two thousand people. A visible shaking was manifested among the dry bones; the Spirit of God descended with power and, from the depths of many previously hard but now broken and contrite hearts, there arose the anxious cry, 'Lord Jesus, save me! O Jesus, come and take away my hard and stony heart!' There were nearly thirty cases of prostration. These people were removed a little distance and, at the same moment, but without the slightest disorder or interruption to each other, might be heard one of the youthful strangers delivering his errand of mercy and telling from the depths of a full heart what

Jesus had done for his own soul. There were groups from which ascended the pleadings for still deeper contrition or mercy and, from others, songs of praise to redeeming love.

"As Mr. White's congregation is a large and widely scattered one, meetings were held in rural districts on the extreme boundaries of it – on Wednesday morning at Gleslick and, though there was a Fair at a distance of a mile, there was a large attendance, another the same evening at Cliffin and the following morning at Cappy; at all of which there were cases of conviction and prostration. On Thursday evening, long before the appointed hour – six o'clock – Mr. White's meeting house was filled to overflowing – not even standing room in the aisles; forms had been provided, the windows thrown open and those who were unable to gain admittance listened to the proclamation of the glad tidings of great joy.

"Mr. White opened the meeting with praise and prayer and the reading of a short portion of scripture. A most touchingly impressive prayer was then offered up by a boy of fourteen, to his Father in Heaven, with all the confidence of a child to a loving, indulgent parent. 'O Father, we expect great things tonight. Disappoint us not for Jesus' sake.' The prayer of faith was not to be unanswered or the promise unfulfilled. 'Whatsoever ye ask the Father in My Name, He will give it you'; for scarcely had Mr. Herron commenced speaking when conviction and prostration began, one and another were removed during the whole of his deeply impressive address. When that was over, before Mr. Patterson had concluded his prayer for the Divine blessing and outpouring of the Holy Spirit, a heart-rending and agonising cry for mercy arose simultaneously from almost every part of the house. It was a truly glorious meeting. There were nearly a hundred cases of prostration, the sighs of many more of silent conviction. After they had found peace, their entreaties were most earnest that they may not be removed from the place where they had found 'sweet Jesus'.

"One of several touching scenes that we witnessed was one poor girl who had been left to stay at home and take care of two children, while the other members attended the meeting. The poor child (she was about nine years of age) could not resist the desire of coming to see what Jesus would do for her soul. Deterred by no false shame she came, though she had neither shoes nor bonnet, and brought the two children with her. To gain admission was then impossible, but she sat down outside with the infant on her knee. She was very soon prostrated. Two of her brothers, one older, the other younger, were attracted by the cries, came near and found it was their sister. Before many minutes she was rejoicing in the peace that 'passeth all understanding,' and there she poured out her soul, her whole soul in supplication for every member of her family. Her two brothers became affected and there the three lay prostrate with their arms entwined around each other's necks and from the lips of that poor uneducated child came a practical lesson on the vanities of the world and the value of the soul, that penetrated the heart of some who heard it. It was pronounced in a voice scarcely audible but so sweetly calm that it deeply impressed some who had before witnessed many thrilling, interesting scenes.

"A prayer meeting had been started in the congregation about one year ago, by the young men who met one evening in the week for prayer and the study of the scriptures. Their prayers were earnest and fervent that God would pour out His Holy Spirit upon this portion of His Son's vineyard, and own and abundantly bless the faithful and untiring labours of their beloved pastor. Truly, 'prayer moves the Hand that moves the universe', and it was, we feel sure, reviving to that pastor's heart to feel that he had not laboured in vain, nor spent his strength for nought, but as case after case under conviction was carried out there was a faithful band who were not ashamed to own their Lord, ready to attend to them and speak, pray or praise God without other feelings than those of fervent gratitude, even before the thronging multitude. It was three o'clock on Friday morning before they could be prevailed on to leave.

"A meeting took place at eleven o'clock on Friday, which lasted to six o'clock in the evening. It was intended only for those under conviction, but the house was quite full. After Mr. White had opened the meeting, his fifth son ascended the pulpit and told his own story – how the Spirit of God found him and now made him – then, looking round on the vast number of familiar faces, he poured out his whole heart in an appeal at once so pathetic, heartfelt and fervent that there was not a creature in the house who was not melted to tears. In fact, the interest is deepening and widening to such an extent, and each meeting so much more crowded than the preceding ones that, if it were not for this incident and hearty co-operation of the young men in connection with the 'Prayer Meeting and Mutual Improvement Society' – one of which we should delight in seeing in connection with every congregation in the assembly, and which the sixth and last son of Mr. White was instrumental in establishing here, and who already has been the instrument of doing so much good – the work could not be carried on, nor those affected attended to as they have been.

"A very striking feature we notice is the more love they feel to Christ, the more love they feel to one another. Another characteristic is the love they bear towards those who were the means of impressing them – there is a felt brotherhood and sisterhood in Christ. Grateful and affectionate glances beam from every eye on the youthful strangers who have been so largely honoured and blessed. Altogether there is so much joy, heartiness and life in everything and with everyone that the most sceptical have been forced to admit there is a reality in it – nothing less than the Spirit of the living God."

"The Ballymena Observer" Saturday, 20th August 1859

Ballycarry

"The refreshing dew of the Holy Spirit is still falling upon us. That cloud of mercy inflated with Heaven's choicest treasure which, in its onward and brightening chorus, visited our district some two months ago, still continues to pour upon us showers of blessings. Though the manifestations are not as so numerous as before, the presence and converting graces of the blessed Spirit are powerfully and effectually experienced by many. The attendance at religious worship is still on the increase and there is, so far as man sees, an almost universal enquiry, 'What shall we do to be saved?'

"On Monday evening the Rev. Mr. Watson preached on the 'Fairgreen' to a large and mostly attentive audience, when a scoffer, supported by a few youths, brought out from his residence a big drum. During the solemn period of praise and prayer walked about the congregation beating it violently, exceedingly mad, as many are towards God's work in the conversion of souls. Ballycarry could not have produced a second character to act in a similar way."

"The Banner of Ulster" Tuesday, 23rd August 1859

"In the Great George's Street Presbyterian Church, the work of God continues to go on in a wonderful manner. On Sabbath the house was filled both morning and evening, and at the latter service some of the people were in the pulpit. An interesting circumstance marked the prayer meeting at the close. An invitation was given to all who were willing to give up their sins and give their hearts to God to kneel in silent prayer, and those who were not willing were requested to stand while the others poured forth their desires to God for mercy and grace. About three hundred individuals fell upon their knees at once, while about one dozen remained standing.

"In the Berry Street Church, on the past Sabbath, there were many cases of conviction. In the morning some sinners were led to call out for mercy, but in the evening there was a very considerable number of both sexes who were carried out and received proper treatment from the officers of the church. We have heard of one young woman who had retired to bed for the night. Another girl slept with her. At about one o'clock the girl was awakened by the piercing screams, and so loudly did she cry that the people in the neighbouring houses were aroused. Some Christian friends came in and endeavoured to console her by pointing her to the sinner's Friend. She is now rejoicing in the hope of the glory of God. Another young woman retired to bed under conviction not having found peace, and in the night it pleased God to answer her prayers and through the expressions of her joy and gratitude she awoke those who were sleeping in the same house. On Sabbath evening a woman who is a member of the congregation was stricken down, and it was most affecting to witness her thankfulness that her prayers too had been heard and answered. On reaching home, her testimony to Christ made a deep impression on those who crowded in to see her."

County Cavan

"The great wave of religious awakening that has been deeply stirring the rest of Ulster has, at length, reached us. For some time past the prayer meetings of Urcher Presbyterian Church have been attended with more than usual solemnity. Our pastor, the Rev. W. Bell, has been untiring in the glorious work. In his weekly administrations, Sunday School, and visitations, his earnest prayer has been that God would, in His own good time, revive His work among us. And truly he has found in the rich harvest that is now being reaped, that God is the Answerer of prayer.

"On Sabbath last, during an earnest but by no means exciting discourse, whilst his audience was deeply impressed, he witnessed by their sobs and tears how fervently they responded to his appeal – several cases of conviction and prostration occurred. Never was I more agreeably surprised than when I listened to the eloquent pleading of laymen – not a few – who, in language earnest, scriptural, and appropriate, poured forth to the Throne of Grace prayers for the consolation of the stricken ones and for the conviction and conversion of those who have not yet learned how terrible it is 'having no hope, and without God in the world.'

"In the evening of the same day I visited Corglass (1ˢᵗ Bailieborough) and found the large church filled to suffocation and the graveyard filled with anxious worshippers. There could not have been less than two thousand people present. The Rev. P. White opened the meeting with singing and prayer and was followed by his son and Mr. Patterson – recent converts who had very earnestly invited their audience to come to the Throne of Grace, in full confidence that the same Jesus Who had done so much for their souls would have mercy upon them. Mr. Thomas R. White had scarcely commenced speaking when simultaneously from various parts of the dense audience there arose the recurring cry of anguish and despair. As a lady well remarked, the place might aptly be compared to 'a house on fire with the doors shut.' Soon the graveyard was covered with numerous groups around the prostrate convicted ones. Some were teaching the way of salvation to poor Romanists, who appeared utterly helpless, uttering nothing but sobs or, 'My sins! My sins!' Others were listening to the earnest, scarcely audible pleadings of those who, all unconscious of what was passing around them, kept whispering:– 'Blessed Jesus! My Saviour! My sweet Saviour!'

"One case I can never forget – a girl about twelve years of age in a retired part of the churchyard with a group of comforters around her and that strange frantic look on her brow and cheek and that light in the eye, peculiar to those in her rapped state, kept sobbing:– 'My sins! My sins! O, the dark cloud of sins, of my long forgotten sins! My God, my God! O, I forgot there was a God!' A strong man listening to her seemed struck, as if it were by a gunshot and, with heaving chest and bloodshot eyes, screamed out for mercy. At ten o'clock, all around that otherwise secluded and peaceful churchyard, was one veil of sorrow and weeping. Mr. M. – the most extensive spirit merchant in County Cavan – under deep conviction of sin has renounced the trade for ever, believing it accursed of God and the downfall of his fellow creatures. He has been paying income tax on a trade of four hundred pound per annum. Old feuds and sectarian animosities are forgotten. The Episcopalian clergy of Bailieborough, Killinkere, and Bellasis are earnest in the movement.

"On Thursday a most interesting meeting took place in Urcher (2nd Bailieborough), resided over by the Rev. W. Bell. Messrs. White and Patterson, in their usual forcible style, invoked the aid of the Holy Spirit. Soon the same heart-stirring cry rang through the assembly, and another, and another were carried out under conviction to receive comfort and peace through the prayers of themselves or their fellow converts. The sceptic and the philosopher are utterly confounded whilst listening to the words of babes in knowledge and in years."

"The Banner of Ulster" Thursday, 25th August 1859

The Moral Effects of the Revival

"A most remarkable incident regarding the moral effects of the revival may be noticed. The 12th August is the Fair Day of Dunnalong – the Donnybrook of the North. In past years this Fair used to be frequented by vagabonds of every type and class, and the idle and vicious from this city and the surrounding county assembled in great force to drink, dance, fight and gamble. Party fights were the rule, and murderous assaults, robberies and debauchery characterised this rural Fair, which was held on both sides of the Foyle.

"On the 12th August 1859, as on former years, the Fair was held for the sale of horses principally. Business was conducted in an ordinary manner. There was no riot, no drunkenness and not a single tent for the sale of whiskey was to be seen on the Greenhill side of County Donegal, which so often had been the scene of drunken brawl between rivals and rebellious, while, from the County Tyrone side of the Foyle, the sweet melody of the Psalms of David arose from the verdant meadowland and was borne over the waters of the Foyle to the opposite shore, from the open-air service that was being held by the esteemed minister of Donagheady. This service was well attended by the country people. Two publicans in the neighbourhood of Dunnalong have given up the sale of spirits and other strong drinks, and this not from any pressure from without, but from conscientious feelings that they were engaged in a sinful, degrading and soul-destroying traffic. Formerly, a party of strolling players about this season of the year used to establish themselves in the village of Carrigans, a few miles from Londonderry, making several pounds sterling weekly from the people during their stay. This season they fixed their location in Carrigans as usual but they were forced to leave – only one man entered the miserable play box and the stage manager handed back to this solitary patron of the legitimate drama his money and moved away to a less enlightened and less religious locality."

"The Ballymena Observer" Saturday, 27th August 1859

"On the evening of Monday the 15th, an elderly man was quietly returning from his daily labour towards his place of residence, not far from Ballymena, when he picked up a scrap of printed paper which he found lying on the road. It proved to be the fragment of a newspaper. Some crumpled words arrested his attention and encouraged him to read as much as it contained of a certain paragraph, ending with the following sentence, 'To you who are engulfed in sin, whose crimes are heaped up like a volcanic mountain around you threatening to pour down a molten stream of vengeance upon your head – to you, reader, even to you is the word of this salvation sent.'

"There is nothing new in the form of these words, nor the way that they were conveyed. The figure of speech implored must be very familiar to everybody but, as strange as it may appear, this accidental or rather providential meeting with it affected the old man exceedingly. His blood suddenly ran cold, his hands trembled, his knees became feeble. In short, conviction fell upon him and he tottered into an adjoining field where he fell with his face towards the earth, and lay unseen by mortal eye in great weakness of body and agony of spirit for about one hour. On reaching home, which he did with great difficulty, he retired to his bed and remained there for two entire days, and then arose from it 'a humble Christian and altered man.'

"These are his own words to us and we have his authority for public reference to this very striking case of sudden conviction on the condition that names are not given in connection with it – for even the members of the man's own family are not aware of all the facts of the occurrence. He has carefully preserved the scrap of paper which, under providence, had arrested him while in a career of recklessness. He handed it over to us for our inspection. It was blotted all over as he had shed many tears. We recognised it instantly.

"It was a fragment of 'The Ballymena Observer', the 5th of March, containing about a quarter of a column of our 'words to the working classes' under the title of 'An Old Story' which (as we then acknowledged) to a large extent was copied from an article that had been arranged and delivered as a lecture to poor men by an English clergyman. It conveys to us that there is something calculated to awaken serious reflection in the 'chain of chances' which led to this extraordinary result.

"Let us review the facts. An English clergyman happened, by chance, to write a certain foreword; the book containing it was purchased in Manchester by a chance visitor from Ballymena; a chance accident occurred to it, and it was brought to this office to be rebound; we opened it, by mere chance, and it occurred to our minds that our column lectures are a similar style of message; by chance it did some good among the labouring classes of this community; by chance it happened that we had an unoccupied column of 'The Observer' and by chance we selected 'An Old Story' and reprinted it; some chance purchaser may have provided himself with a copy of the paper; months afterwards it was torn up for some chance purpose, and a fragment of it was dropped by chance upon a public road; the wind drifted it by chance to the foot of a person; and by another chance the traveller saw with fancy to pick it up. The 'chances' ended there! The purpose of providence had been accomplished by a series of second causes.

"Further proof that parties are frequently suddenly convicted without any externally exciting cause, we may observe that a woman apparently of full age fell down in one of the pews at morning service in the Parochial Church on Sunday last and alarmed the congregation by a piercing cry that God would pardon her at that moment when the clergyman was quietly engaged in reading the first Bible lesson of the day.

"A great variety of similar cases are before us but, for the present, we pass them in order to make room for the following details of a remarkable conversion, noted down precisely as stated to us in an interview with this person on Monday last. We have no personal knowledge of the young man, but he called at this office with letters of introduction from two gentlemen of respectability to whom he is known and who are generally aware of the leading facts:-

"'I was born in the neighbourhood of Londonderry, and have lived the greater part of my life there where I am well known. I am now eighteen years of age and, until two months ago, I was never able to speak so that I could be understood. I was not dumb but was born with some natural impediment which, during all the previous part of my life, deprived me of the power of intelligible utterance. I had been taught to work as a stone mason and, until two months ago, I was a Roman Catholic, a drunkard and, so far as my will was concerned and my stammering permitting it, I was a blasphemer. I was so bad a character as any man could be, for I was not in Christ.

"'Some time ago I went to work at Moneymore, in employment of Daniel Magee. When the revival movement commenced there I used to go to some of the meetings, but it was only to hang about the outskirts and mock at the people – I took no other interest in them for my heart was hardened. Shortly after midnight on Sunday the 19th June last I was passing the open door of a private home in Moneymore, in which the Rev. Dr. Barnett was engaged in prayer. I had no intention of going in but was right opposite the door. I heard the Rev. Gentleman saying some words about the Lord Jesus, which attracted my curiosity. A power, which I firmly believe to have been exercised by the Spirit of God upon me, inclined me to go in. I entered and was not long in the house until I knelt with the people of it, but my heart was not touched.

"'When Rev. Dr. Barnett left the house I followed him along the street. I did not want to speak with him, but I felt an impulse to proceed with him to another house where the people wanted him to pray. Just then some weakness – some strange feeling that I was unable to explain – came over me. I could not stand, and I fell prostrate upon the street. Up to that moment I had no thought about religion, or the state of my soul and I had not been excited by anything, or in any way.

"'It was just after I had fallen that the Spirit of God – and I am confident it was nothing else – put the feeling into my heart that I was a sinner, lost and perishing, and that my only hope of salvation was in Christ. I felt a deep conviction of that and a terror of mind that no words could describe. I did not become insensible and all the while I felt a weight about my heart as if something were crushing me through the heart. This was about one o'clock in the morning and some people carried me into the house of James Beattie. I resided there 'til five o'clock in the morning before I was able to walk to the home in which I lodged.

"'I could not speak, but my heart prayed to the Lord Jesus. I was brought to believe, to my great comfort, that a good work had begun in me under the influence of the Holy Spirit. I felt peace of mind, a firm faith in my Redeemer and a confident trust that His power would protect and guide me to final salvation. Since that time I have had unbounded confidence and comfort in Christ. I have not had any return of illness. I have neither doubt nor fear of mind and I continue in earnest and humble prayer that my faith in Him may be strengthened day by day.

"'For the first six hours after one o'clock on the night of that Monday I lay quiet. I did not try to speak. I did not know that I could speak, and cannot tell whether I could have spoken if I had tried. At the end of that time, blessed be God, I found that the power of perfect speech had been bestowed on me and that I, who had never before spoken a plain word in all my life, could now praise

His Name without impediment. I had received a new tongue, a new heart and new desires. Old things had passed away and all things became new to me.

"'For six years before, I was a drunkard and also dreadfully addicted to the excessive use of tobacco. I was either smoking it or chewing it almost continually. I always went to bed, and to sleep, with tobacco in my mouth and I could not sleep without it. I have not the slightest inclination either for it, or intoxicating drink now, nor ever had from the hour of my wonderful restoration to speech, and rescue from the dominion of Satan by an Almighty Power. I thank and praise God for that conversion and I can never be sufficiently thankful for it.

"'I was a Roman Catholic. I am not one now nor ever shall be again. From the first moment that I felt the Hand of God upon me, and the influence of the Holy Spirit upon my heart, I refused to allow anyone to bring a Priest to me. In former days I thought over some prayers used to invoke the aid of saints of the Virgin Mary. But now the Lord has taught me to pray from the heart. I feel that it is sin to put any creative being in the room of that blessed Saviour, Who died for me, that I might live. If man could work out his own salvation by penitence or good works, he might go a conqueror to Heaven in his own right, where man never yet entered except as a conqueror 'through Him that loved us'.

"'I have not yet joined myself to any particular Protestant denomination, for they are all brethren in Christ; but I have had gospel consolation and instruction from the kind attention of the Rev. Dr. Barnett, and the Rev. Mr. Sinclair. I have been at a good many revival meetings where I have used the speech which God has given me in telling what he has done for my soul. I know of a good many converts from the Roman Catholic religion and, in particular, of a young man called J.P. who used to attend the Priest. In the service of the Mass many others who have been taught with me upon the subject appeared to be in great doubt. I am now on the way to my native place of Londonderry and have letters of introduction and character from the clergymen of Moneymore, to the Rev. Dr. Denham and other gentlemen of the city and neighbourhood. I certify the entire truth of this statement which I authorise and request you to publish as encouragement to some, as warning to others and for the glory of God. David Creswell.'

"We offer no commentary on the above case. The facts are fairly before the public, and we leave everyone to judge for himself in respect of the cause of the character and result."

"The Armagh Guardian" Tuesday, 30th August 1859

Mall Church, Armagh

"The services last Sabbath were deeply solemn and instructive. Mr. Kimmit of London preached a most admirable sermon on the words, 'Men ought always to pray,' and in the evening Mr. McAllister considered and answered the objections raised against the present revival of religion. Mr. Geddis of Sandholes, on Monday evening, addressed the prayer meeting, which was large, in a clear, able and truly impressive manner. Good was done. Several left the meeting under deep conviction. Many felt that the drops of the shower of mercy were falling. It fell in a plenteous shower on Tuesday upon the daily schools – the children in the Sabbath School of this church had a similar precious visitation of the Holy Spirit on Sabbath last.

"A number retired from the Sabbath School shedding tears about the state of their souls. Mr. McAllister met to pray with them in another and quieter place, and one intelligent and interesting girl could not restrain herself and cried out. Many had been weeping before but now the lamentation over sin and the cry to the Lord Jesus for mercy was loud and long. While the Rev. James Stevenson of Ayr was preaching for Mr. McAllister he, and several of his Sabbath School teachers, were attending to the children under conviction of sin. It was a quickening, refreshing and happy scene when, after the public service, Mr. Stevenson and several parents came to the place where the Holy Spirit was working amidst the children, to witness the Lord's marvellous kindness. Hearts were filled with the most joyous emotions. Earnest prayers were offered up and more than one Psalm of gratitude was sung. This is the Lord's doing and marvellous in our eyes – one of the most precious and heart-melting scenes ever witnessed in this city was seen.

"A little girl entered the female school at about eleven o'clock saying:– 'Oh! I have found Jesus.' In a moment another little girl screamed out and fell. The Holy Spirit moved over them. In a short time there was a loud and almost universal wail. The boys rushed into the females' school. A boy ran to Mr. McAllister and met him in the street and cried to him:– 'Come, come, Sir, the girls in the school are all crying for mercy.' When he entered, some were on their knees, some were lying in the arms of the teacher, some in the arms of other children, floods of tears were flowing, confession of sin was made from little broken hearts, cries for mercy from God – for Jesus to come and save them – for the Holy Spirit to print the image of Jesus upon their hearts – for the Lord to take away the stony heart out of their flesh and give them a heart of flesh. Providentially, the Rev. Ferguson of Alwyth was in Mr. McAllister's home and was able to help in the blessed work most ably. The Rev. Messrs. Smith and Henderson by and by came with a great many others and saw this most sublime sight."

"The Banner of Ulster" Saturday, 3rd September 1859

Armagh

"In the 1st Presbyterian Church many souls are daily finding peace at the cross of Christ. On Sabbath morning last the Spirit's presence was greatly manifested in the Sabbath School. Many of the children and young persons of both sexes left the church with the solemn words on their lips:– 'Lord, save me or I perish.' A great number of those are now able to say:– 'I am happy in Christ.' After the morning service in the church last Lord's day an effecting scene was witnessed in the retiring room. Eight persons were all on their knees at the same time wrestling in intense agony of prayer to Christ to save their souls. Four of these were of the same family – three brothers and a sister. Besides them were kneeling their father – a godly man – and two sisters who had already known Jesus to be 'the way, the truth, and the life.' Within a minute or two, two of the brothers exclaimed:– 'Blessed Jesus!' 'Sweet Saviour!' It was then that the scene was truly sublime – the meeting of a father with two newborn sons of God. On last Sabbath morning affectionate addresses were delivered to them by the Rev. Messrs. Stevenson and McAllister. One and another cried for forgiveness. The scene was solemnizing. To see so many young people in deep agony for their sins, praying to God for the Redeemer's sake to have mercy upon them and, after a time, the Lord lifting up the light of His countenance upon them and giving them peace and joy, was indeed solemnising and joyful."

Moneyreagh

"On Sabbath evening last, the 28th, the Rev. J. M. Killen, Comber, preached to an immense assembly in the open-air near the Unitarian Meeting House, Moneyreagh. It has been calculated by those qualified to judge that upwards of five thousand people must have been present. The vast audience listened with profound attention to the preacher for upwards of two hours and during the service a great number of prostrations took place. At the end of the service the place surrounding the locality where the service had been held was dotted over by groups engaged in attending to the convicted ones and who administered instruction or consolation as the cases required. Altogether the scene was most interesting and solemnising, and God's children who were present considered that the cause of revival received great encouragement from the services in which they had been engaged. Rev. Killen was earnestly requested to hold a similar service next Sabbath evening, but other engagements prevent him from immediately complying with their requests."

Drum, County Monaghan

"The revival movement, like a mighty wave, has spread far and wide over this district. At the regular prayer meetings held in 2nd Drum Presbyterian Meeting House on Wednesday week it pleased the Lord to visit us by His mighty Spirit, prostrating to the earth under conviction of sins some thirty or forty individuals and as many more on their way home and in their houses, and subsequently filling their souls with a sense of pardon, peace and joy through faith in their crucified Saviour. At our meeting on Wednesday last a similar but more abundant outpouring of the Spirit descended upon us, assembled as we then were among the graves of the departed dead. In a moment, amid the stillness and suppressed sobs of the multitude and at a time when prayer was being offered up (and consequently when there was no excitement), were heard here and there throughout the vast assembly cries of mercy becoming louder and louder. More than sixty or seventy people of all sexes and ages at the meeting, and twice as many more during the night, were alike constrained to cry out in agony for pardon and forgiveness through the blood and sacrifice of Jesus.

"Familiar manifestations have also appeared in the other houses of worship. Careless, prayerless sinners have now become serious and prayerful. There is not one Protestant house within two miles in each direction of the village of Drum in which family worship is not now observed night and morning, and in some houses three times each day. Truly, the religious feeling which prevails the people now is quite sufficient to trample beneath it the gigantic kingdom of vice that Satan has so long reared in this neighbourhood. Profaning the Sabbath has ceased here. The very people who were once guilty of violating the Lord's Day are among the persons whom God has raised up to denounce the sinful practice! Where is the man now who would enter a public house, as was usual before on the Sabbath, and sit and drink and obliterate the good impressions made on his mind by the preaching of God's truth?

"Verily, public opinion through the mighty Spirit of God has trampled into the dust the kingdom of Satan in this neighbourhood and, instead of the mass of people being ashamed of Christ and of religion, they are now ashamed of Satan and Satan's kingdom, which has fallen into ruins under this renovating influence of the Spirit of God Who can make 'all things new'. Blessed be God that we have lived to see these days! To see the mouths of our Sabbath School children open in prayer! To hear on Sabbath evenings, instead of the godless laugh and the sinful jest, every house a house of prayer, and every lip a lip of praise! To hear on market evenings, when formerly the echo of blasphemy and drunken cries reverberated from the heavens, now nothing but the sobs of the heavy laden sinner or else the song of praise ascending from the sanctified lips and hearts! To see our places of worship filled to overflowing and the people of every Protestant denomination enquiring their way to Zion with their faces hitherward! Surely the faithful of all denominations have good reason now to adopt the sentiments of the Psalmist and to say:– 'The LORD hath done great things for us; whereof we are glad.'"

"The Ballymena Observer" Saturday 3rd September 1859

Remarkable Incident – Revival at Sea

"One of the most extraordinary and interesting incidents, which has occurred since the commencement of the revival took place on Friday night last. While the mail steamer, "The Stag" was on her trip from Belfast to Glasgow, a number of the passengers, among whom were Brownlow North, a number of ministers of the Free Church and a Christian gentleman from Belfast assembled on the quarterdeck about half past eleven, after the vessel had cleared the Lough and was fairly out in the channel. The night was beautifully clear and quite calm – the surface of the sea almost like a mirror.

"The conversation among the group turned to the great work which the Spirit is accomplishing in the North of Ireland. The Belfast gentleman remarked that he had witnessed displays of the awakening influence, accompanied by physical symptoms of deep conviction, among members of every evangelical denomination with one exception – that of the Society of Friends.

"At the very time when this conversation was going on, a young man ascended the quarterdeck and respectfully approached the people standing together there and said, 'A young woman at the front of the ship has been stricken down'. The group immediately proceeded to the portion of the vessel indicated, and found a young girl leaning against some packages of merchandise surrounded by a number of people who seemed deeply interested in her condition. It was soon recognised that she was not only a native of Ireland, but – a strange coincidence – a member of the Society of Friends. She had been convicted of sin at a religious meeting a few evenings before and was so overwhelmed by a sense of the danger of her soul that she was constrained to cry out for mercy then and there and, by the Divine blessing, also found it.

"At the request of some ministers of the Free Church, religious worship was conducted on the deck of the steamer by the gentleman from Belfast already referred to. The 40th Psalm was given out and sung with unusual fervency by the large party assembled. The young girl heartily joined in it. Nothing could be more startling or impressive than the sounds of praise and prayer wafting in the still midnight hour over the wide expansive waters – reminding some who listened to them of Paul and Silas singing in the prison at Philippi. The entire scene indeed formed one of the most solemn and interesting incidents that had been witnessed. Several of the crew of the steamer, who were on watch on deck, joined in the services."

"The Downshire Protestant" Friday, 16th September 1859

Ballynahinch

"For the last two months the Lord's work has been spreading in this place; hundreds, I have reason to believe, have passed through the gate of conversion. Prayer meetings have been established here in every district and are conducted by the young and old of the neighbourhood. Let a minister be seen passing anywhere during the last three weeks and going into a house and, in a few minutes, the reapers would be seen leaving the fields and thronging the house such is their unquenchable thirst for the means of grace. There have been some conversions of Roman Catholics.

"One, for instance, who has joined the Rev. Mr. Davis' Presbyterian congregation was convicted in her own garden; she prayed, although she was nineteen years of age and her mother beat her severely for doing so. She fled from the house but, on a promise of kinder treatment from her parents and by the advice of the Rev. Mr. Davis, she went back and while she was at home she was heard by the family to pray 'like a Protestant.' Her mother pulled her out of bed and told her to say the 'Hail Mary.' On refusing to do this her mother again beat her severely, her father kicked her and her sister struck her with a spade. In consequence of this treatment she has left them and attends the Rev. Mr. Davis' church regularly and gives all the signs of being a consistent Protestant.

"For the last few weeks there has not been so many physical manifestations of the revival, but on the last Sabbath, as if in answer to the fervent prayers of many, all the churches were visited by a Divine blessing in the number of converts made. Boorns Circus was here last week, but few went near it and so irritated were the men connected with it that they joined with a number of Roman Catholics in singing profane songs while the congregations were passing to and from the churches. As a set off to this, however, one

Roman Catholic was heard to say a few days ago to some people who were speaking against the revival:– 'You may talk of the revival as you like, but it has done more against the public houses here than ever Father Martin could do.' On the whole a new impulse has been given to the work in this neighbourhood and converts have been made in two-thirds of the Presbyterian and other Protestant families of the country. In a Dromara neighbourhood the work progresses as much as here and especially amongst the members of the Rev. Messrs. Rutgers and Craig's congregations."

"The Banner of Ulster" Saturday, 17th September 1859

Ballyboley

"Even into this wild and mountainous district of County Antrim – notable formerly and chiefly for the number of game it breeds and the numbers of poachers who made them their own, despite all the regulations to the contrary – the revival has found its way. Formerly there was scarcely a man or a boy in the whole district who was not a poacher – skillful, expert and proud of this contraband craft. At the present moment we are informed by a gentleman who owns a large portion of the grounds and is anxious that the game should be preserved, not a feather is touched by those who previously left the moors bearing grouse and plover. So well assured is the landlord of the sincerity of his former erratic tenants in this respect that he can even entrust a hamper of wine in their way without fear of raid."

Maghera

"The work of the Spirit is more apparent in this town and neighbourhood at present than during any former period. In the absence of any physical excitement whatsoever there are people brought under conviction every day followed nearly in every case, so far as man can judge, by a change of heart and life. Prayer meetings are held every evening, and scarcely a meeting passes without someone being brought under conviction or some anxious enquirer being enabled to lay hold of Christ. Christians here have zeal, but it is a good cause – it is for the conversion of souls and not for the encouragement of extravagance of any kind that might tend to mar the real work of God, or lead pious and shrewd men to doubt that there is a great work of God going on at present. As yet we have seen no cases of deafness or dumbness, nor have we talked with any person who has said he has seen a vision, and we trust we shall be long so as we have no desire at present for new revelations. The scriptures state, 'If they hear not Moses and the prophets, neither will they be persuaded, though one rose from the dead.'"

"The Ballymena Observer" Saturday, 17th September 1859

"To every intelligent observer of local occurrences connected with the revival it must appear obvious that the most important and extensive social, moral and religious improvements have already been affected among the community. New cases of 'impression' occurred at divine services in all the evangelical churches of Ballymena on Sunday last. Fresh impulse has been given to the good work by the proceedings at an open-air meeting held in the Linenhall (and Market Place) on the following Tuesday. This meeting excited unusual interest because of an announcement that it would conclude the outdoor services for the present season. By eleven o'clock in the forenoon every thoroughfare leading to the hall was crowded with people of both sexes and of every rank and age - nearly everyone of them being provided with a copy of the Sacred Volume. Much rain had fallen in the course of the preceding night but, towards morning, the weather became better and continued to be highly favourable throughout the entire day.

"The spacious hall, a quadrangular enclosure surrounded by forty or 50 offices for the use of linen merchants, was crowded to excess. A considerable amount of the audience obtained an advantageous position in the adjoining building from the open windows, from which the speakers could be distinctly heard. Seats with accommodation for about two thousand people had been provided in the open hall, but the entire assembly fully doubled that number, and a more deeply attentive audience to proceedings of great earnestness we have never witnessed.

"Among the audience we noticed a number of Roman Catholics who conducted themselves with the most creditable attention to propriety, and also several respectable members of the Unitarian Church who appeared to take a deep interest in the worship. In the course of the proceedings we observed that several people of both sexes were affected to tears. A number of them were assisted from the meeting, or were obliged to retire to some of the neighbouring offices, evidently in great weakness of body and aggravation of mind."

Great Revival Meeting at Armagh

"On Wednesday, according to previous announcements which had been widely made known throughout the district of the county, a revival meeting was held in Armagh. One of the leading objects of the meeting was to bring together the friends of the movement from the neighbouring counties in order that a concentrated effort might be made for its extension. Friends of the cause in Belfast entered into arrangements with the Ulster Railway Company for running a special train yesterday morning to Armagh. This was placed under the direction of Mr. Revell. The scene at the Belfast terminal of the Ulster Railway shortly after nine o'clock yesterday morning was one of an unusual and exciting experience. The weather was exceedingly fine – there was a bright warm sunshine, with every prospect that this would continue throughout the day.

"Notwithstanding the excellent efforts which had been made to secure sufficient accommodation for the large number of people who, it was understood, would attend the Armagh meeting – it was only after a set of carriages had been attached together, when the length of the train extended from the extremity of the rails in the station to Linfield Mill, that people desirous of procuring seats could obtain them.

"About a quarter of an hour after the appointed time the immense train took its departure. The carriages then contained between three thousand and four thousand people, and it was at once seen that great difficulty would be felt in arranging accommodation for people who were waiting its arrival at other stations. At Lisburn there was a large number of passengers assembled and these, with much pushing and squeezing, obtained seats.   At Moira, the same scene was repeated but not with like results.

"Prior to arriving at that station every seat had been filled, but the people were so intent upon proceeding on the journey that they mounted on to the roofs of the carriages, despite the remonstrations of the officials who anticipated great danger from their position while the train would be passing under the bridges along the line. In the midst of the natural excitement which ensued, all that the officers of the Company could do was to warn the people on the top of each carriage to throw themselves flat while passing beneath the bridges. We are glad to be able to say that this advice was strictly attended to, and the consequence was the avoidance of accidents.

"After leaving Moira it was wisely decided that the train should not stop until it arrived at Portadown – leaving to the regular train, which followed at ten o'clock, the duty of picking up a very large group assembled at Lurgan. At Portadown, some additional carriages were attached. These were at once filled and, after a quarter of an hour delay, the large train proceeded on its journey and arrived at Armagh about one o'clock.

"While noticing this part of the day's proceedings we should refer to a most remarkable feature of the trip to and from Armagh, which attracted considerable attention – especially from English and Scottish clergymen, and others from a distant part of the United Kingdom. While the train was on its way, the sound of voices engaged in singing well known revival hymns arose from almost every carriage.

"While at the several stations large numbers of tracts were extensively circulated. In the carriage in which we ourselves travelled the whole topic of conversation was the present religious movement and when this was not going on respectably dressed young men employed themselves in singing 'What's the News?', while one or two women occasionally read a portion of the scriptures. The scene was one of the most remarkable character, and will not soon pass from the memory of those who witnessed it.

"On arriving at Armagh all the elements of a great meeting presented themselves. There had been special trains from Monaghan, Dungannon and other places, and the town appeared to be completely filled by masses of people all dressed in Sabbath attire – belonging to the several sections of the Protestant Church in the Counties of Armagh, Monaghan and Antrim. No more suitable spot for holding the meeting could have been chosen than that which had been obtained.

"It was a large field immediately adjoining the Railway Station, and we believe it had been placed at the disposal of the promoters of the movement in that town by the proprietor, Mr. Stanley. The field occupied a considerable elevation so that the beautiful country in the vicinity, under an almost cloudless sky, was seen to the very best advantage. A platform had been erected for the speakers, and around this the immense crowd gathered. It is difficult to come to anything like an exact estimate of the number of people on the field but, after making some enquiries on the subject, we think there could not have been less than twenty thousand people at the services during the day. It was gratifying also to remark that these included a large number of the higher class of Armagh and its neighbourhood, as well as the intelligent farmers with their wives and families belonging to the three Counties we have named.

"There were present also a very large body of clergymen connected with various evangelical denominations – a perfect list of whose names it was impossible to obtain, especially of those gentlemen from England and Scotland who are now in this country collecting information on the progress of the work of the revival.

"The Rev. Baptist W. Noel was introduced to the meeting, and spoke at considerable length. He took for the basis of his address the fact that the Lord Jesus Christ was ready to save the immortal souls of sinners, and that they themselves were to blame if they did not ultimately meet with salvation. On this topic he spoke with fervent simplicity, which we rarely have heard equalled. He expressed the great delight which he felt at being privileged to attend such an immense meeting as it was, and he thanked God that the souls of the people had been awakened to a sense of their need.

"If in the multitude, he said, that was before him, there was one unconverted soul – and he was sure there were many – now was the time to approach the Throne of Grace – now was the time to approach the Heavenly Father Who, through the intercession of the Saviour, was willing and ready to forgive the transgressions of their past lives. If they only appealed to Him with a true spirit. He addressed himself to the young and to the old – he addressed himself to those who were upon the noontide of life, and to those who were on the brink of the grave – and he earnestly beseeched them to avail themselves of this glorious opportunity to make their peace with God.

"He trusted that, with the blessing of God, this movement would not be confined to Ireland but that it would spread itself among the great intellects of England, and that men would see, at length, in a true and sincere spirit that they had souls to be saved. It might be a strange thing that the North of Ireland and its people should become the great heralds of this movement. However, he believed that if they exercised their influence they might do much to extend the influence of God's Kingdom and Glory.

"Mr. Ernest Noel (the son of Rev. Baptist W. Noel) applied a happy influence among the audience with which he mingled. One or two of these instances, which came within our own notice, are worthy of being recorded. Mr. Noel, in the course of mixing with several groups assembled in the field, met with two people who had evidently attended with the object of turning the meeting into a time of ridicule. They belonged to the lower classes. They paid no respect to the religious worship going on and treated the proceedings with apparent contempt. He considered that the opportunity should not be lost sight of and entered into a friendly conversation with them, learned their opinions kindly and earnestly and gently remonstrated with them. He laid before them some gospel truths and, to the most superficial observer, it was evident that both of the people he addressed left his presence not only wiser but better men.

"In another instance we observed Mr. Noel in company with a soldier belonging to the troops stationed in Armagh. This man had seen some hotly contested engagements for he bore on his breast three medals and several clasps. Mr. Noel remarked that he always liked to see the colour of a red coat, and he liked to be able to find that every man who wore a red coat had the certainty of salvation. The reply was, 'We usually pray for the dead – not the living.' 'And why not for the living?' asked Mr. Noel. 'Have not the thousands around you souls to be saved? Have you not a soul to be saved yourself? Have not your comrades' souls to be saved? Have we not all souls which must, at some time after this, meet our Heavenly Master?' The soldier confessed the fact, and then Mr. Noel went on to state that he had a friend in military service, an officer at present stationed in Dublin. He was a gallant soldier who was prepared to serve his Queen and Country in any country – he had braved dangers of the most dreadful character, and would face the cannon's mouth, or enter the breach with the courage of any man in the service.

"But, while he was this, he was more than this – he was a soldier of Christ – he was a living witness of God's truth, and this had been to him the greatest comfort and consolation in the hour of battle. The scene between Mr. Noel and this bronzed old soldier was, beyond all question, the most remarkable incident of the day. So familiar, so truly earnest, so strictly conversational was the topic considered on the one hand, and so doubting, so sceptical and, at length, so full of attention was it apparently considered upon the other, that this group formed a picture of the deepest matter for profound thought."

"The Banner of Ulster" Thursday, 22nd September 1859

Dundonald

"On Tuesday evening last the largest prayer meeting which has been held in this neighbourhood since the commencement of the religious awakening took place in Mr. Galway's barn, in the vicinity of Dundonald. The meeting was opened with praise, after which Mr. Chandler expounded a portion of scripture. The subsequent services were conducted by a gentleman from Belfast. During the delivery of the first address a number of persons were stricken down under conviction, all of whom cried earnestly for mercy and most of whom, there is reason to believe, have found it. One young woman in particular seemed to be very deeply impressed. She left the meeting and, some time afterwards, was found on her knees in an adjacent barn and heard to offer up a truly affecting prayer.

"The entire meeting was of the most solemn and interesting kind. A large proportion of those in attendance remained after the close of the regular proceedings, and several of them were engaged in ministering consolation to the stricken ones. Short addresses were delivered by Mr. Chandler and the Christian friend from Belfast, and the meeting was finally brought to a close considerably after the usual hour for terminating such assemblies.

"At the Dundonald station, while several of those who had been at the meeting were waiting the departure of the train, a respectable young woman was observed seated on a form evidently deeply engaged in prayer – her eyes closed and her lips silently moving. After her prayer was finished, a Christian gentleman sat down beside her and entered into conversation on the subject of the religious awakenings and discovered that she was a member of one of the Presbyterian churches in Newtownards, and that she had been brought under spiritual influence during the revival work in that town. She stated that, when first observed, she was seeking grace to strengthen her and for a clearer evidence of her union with Christ. She manifestly was one of the many who had passed from darkness into marvellous light by the power of the Spirit. She stated that during last Sunday, which was communion Sabbath in the Rev. McCullough's church, Newtownards, a large number of people were convicted both during the morning prayer meeting and the midday service, and that the attendance at the communion was the greatest ever known at the ancient church mentioned. Few people of her acquaintance had been reached by the awakening influence who had not been, more or less, brought to a knowledge of the truth."

"The Derry Standard" Saturday, 24th September 1859

Newtownstewart

"A large open-air meeting was held on Thursday the 22nd September in a field adjoining the town of Newtownstewart. It was attended by a great number of people from the neighbouring district. About two hundred converts, and others, left the town of Gortin at twelve o'clock to attend this meeting, walking in procession, headed by the Rev. Matthew Logan. When they were half-way between Gortin and Newtownstewart, they were joined by upwards of three hundred of that congregation headed by their pastor the Rev. Thomas Johnston. Afterwards, on the way to the place of the meeting, they were joined by large numbers. In passing through the town of Newtownstewart there could not have been less than nine hundred to one thousand people in the procession. Those in the procession sang the most popular revival hymns and Psalms the whole way, both going and returning. The meeting commenced at three o'clock, at which time there were upwards of two thousand five hundred people present.

"The meeting was opened by a short but appropriate address and prayer by the Rev. R. C. Donnell. Addresses were delivered by the Rev. F. Little and the Rev. Thomas Johnston. A very edifying lecture was delivered by the Rev. Matthew Logan on the 2nd chapter of Ephesians. The preaching lasted for about one hour. Prayers were offered up by a number of the converts and the above named ministers. There were about ten people openly brought under conviction of their lost and ruined state. There were twenty cases of open conviction in the meeting house besides; many of those thus affected professed to have found peace in Jesus before leaving."

"The Banner of Ulster" Thursday, 6th October 1859

Bangor

"The Rev. S. Nicholson, the minister of the Methodist Church, has written to us as follows:– 'Since my last letter you had inserted for me, we have had some convicted in several meeting houses of this town and some in their own homes. On Sunday the 28th August I preached two sermons to the young converts. One man, J. R., who had been stricken before, fell down in a pew before me and was removed. I had this day some sixty converts present, and many of them had been stricken. God was with us in the power of His Spirit both morning and evening. After I closed the night's service I visited Miss T. who had been stricken again. She seemed as if under demonic possession. She was held, or would undoubtingly have hurt herself. On Monday the 29th I called to see the above female. I found her slightly convulsed and being held. I prayed for her and she became quite calm and composed. We sang hymns to her; two she requested herself. One of them was, 'One There is Above all Others, O how He loves!' I spent more than one hour with her. I left bathed in tears, fully convinced that this is the work of God's Holy Spirit and truth.'

"A young man was convicted on the loom and would have fallen through the web but was caught by his companion. The whole family seemed to be affected and are more fully yielding their hearts to God.

"The following remarkable incident of the power of the Holy Spirit we now bring to the view of our readers. Circumstances prevented its insertion sooner, but now we can add further that the subject of this gracious work has joined himself to the visible Church of Christ, waxing stronger and stronger as he grows in grace and in the knowledge of God. He said to me, who rejoiced with him in his great deliverance out of the land of Egypt:– 'As I was coming up the street last night I prayed to God that I might hear the roars of my wife as I entered the house.' His own 'roars' had been followed by unspeakable happiness, and his love to his wife appeared in praying earnestly for her. 'Blessed are the merciful: for they shall obtain mercy.' Oh that the whole land were crying for mercy!"

The Chimney-Sweep

"A call from a labourer was heard to come and see a man in distress. He was the chimney-sweep of the town – a Roman Catholic who was convicted of sin on the street at nine o'clock and, with his heavy burden, retired steadily to his house. There he lay on his back with hands clasped in agony of supplication and, face turned upwards, he cried mightily, 'Jesus, Jesus have mercy upon me – have mercy upon me. Take, oh take away this hard and stony heart. Oh Jesus come down upon me now – come down upon me now, will You, will You? Oh Jesus, I was mocking. I was mocking yesterday.' When asked, 'Who were you mocking?' He cried in agony, 'It was Jesus. It was Jesus I was mocking. Oh Jesus, take away this hard heart. I confess my sins. I was a wicked sinner from my very infancy. Oh Jesus, Jesus have mercy upon me. I will not go to Hell nor to purgatory but to Jesus – to Jesus. Oh Jesus, I was a Roman Catholic but oh, come to me and I will be no more.' Thus he cried over and over again in agony, the intensity of which no writing can portray.

"No prayer could be better than his, and the wicked were compelled to listen with fear and awe. The presence of others seemed not to be noticed by the man, so wrapped up was he with Jehovah's being and his own sin. What many heard and saw that night, in that poor man's room – this poor man's agony was so great when awakened in this world to the knowledge that there is a God. What must the awakening in Hell be where there is no hope for mercy? Next morning, when asked how he was he replied, 'Better, but I have not got Jesus enough yet.' A labourer who called on the chimney-sweep after the next morning said, 'You were in great distress last night.'

'Oh, yes I was.' he answered. 'I saw myself hanging by a thread over a bottomless pit.' 'Why did you not call to the Virgin in your distress?' 'Oh, no,' shaking his head, 'Jesus is the best.' 'Oh, when men are awakened to know that there is a God, the Virgin, or all virgins, can do them no good – none but Jesus, none but Jesus when it is life or death.'

"We read of Mary in Acts 1:14, who was last seen in a prayer meeting in the upper room, in Jerusalem, as any other poor sinner praying for grace, mercy and peace to her own needy soul. There is no mention made in scripture that Mary ever received the power of the Holy Ghost, as many others had. The Holy Spirit well knew the doctrine of the devil that would spring up, when the mystery of iniquity – the devil's masterpiece – would put a woman – a sinner – in the room and stead of the only Mediator between God and man – the Man Christ Jesus. Those taught of God as that sweep was on Tuesday night know assuredly that Jesus, Jehovah Jesus, can alone help them in the day of their distress when they are brought up out of the grave of spiritual death. None but Jesus will do when they feel themselves hanging by a thread over a bottomless pit or the sparks of Hell fire about them.

"The next night the devil came to the chimney-sweep and offered him anything if he would come with him, and he was in great distress – if not greater than the first night. But he cried to Jesus and, at length, the word came to him with power – 'Arise, Thomas, thy burden is light', and he did rise. The burden fell away. A week afterwards, when spoken to, Thomas said he would not exchange Christ for ten thousand worlds. He feels himself now to be the Lord's chimney-sweep and he will sweep the chimneys better than ever. He has procured a spelling book in order to learn to read, and has worshipped in his house, the wife reading the Bible for him. The Lord came to him on Tuesday night upon the quay as he was about to draw a match to light his pipe. But another light shone in upon his soul, and he fell down prostrate upon the ground as before mentioned. He says he will have nothing more to do with the Virgin or Roman Catholics unless to invite them to come to Jesus. Oh, how wonderful is our God in His doings!

"In Black Bull Close, where Thomas stays, the Lord of Hosts has taken twelve souls 'out of the mouth of the lion and the bear'. It was such a very wicked place that a lady was afraid to accept it as a district for delivering tracts. About two summers ago, a fine young lady died from fever caught whilst engaged in her labour of love in Black Bull Close."

"The Ballymena Observer" Saturday, 8ᵗʰ October 1859

"In the course of the present week, we have been favoured with a variety of communications. From these we select for publication as being, on some points, materially different from any heretofore recorded in this journal. The writer is known to us, but we have no authority to give his name. The communication was received in the form of a letter addressed to ourselves, and the leading particulars will be found in the following extract:–

"'When I was a boy I was familiar with my religious catechism and could repeat every word in it. But I neither understood, nor tried to understand it. The committal of the answers was imposed upon me as a task which, having learnt, I thought I had done quite enough. When I grew older I read the Bible, both at home and at school. I was obliged to read it – but I did not study what I read. I had no desire that the gospel should make me 'wise unto salvation'. When the selection of the chapters was left to myself I always chose those containing the stories about David and Goliath, Saul and the witch at Endor, Samson and the Philistines, the plagues of Egypt and suchlike.

"'At every period of my life I attended divine service almost every Sunday. I was obliged to do so, but I frequently fell asleep there and was always glad to get away and hardly ever remembered anything of the sermon except the text. I never was a scoffer at religion, never a drunkard nor a blasphemer. I never defrauded my neighbour and have always been regarded as a moral man. But I was a mere formalist – in fact, I was 'without God in this world'. Such was my condition when the revival movement became noticeable about Ahoghill in February last – and that movement startled me.

"'In the course of the following three months I witnessed a number of very remarkable cases. They astonished me and, when that feeling subsided, it was succeeded by one of curiosity. I began to investigate the matter more closely – to imagine the causes which produced the effect and regarding the operation as, in all cases, commencing with an influence upon the mind. I then read the Bible with an attention which I had never previously bestowed upon it, in order possibly to understand what cause existed for the mental apprehensions. From this investigation I arose with a distinct perception that all sinners needed a Saviour, and had just cause for alarm as to their future condition in eternity but, up to this time, I did not regard myself as a sinner nor had I perceived any special necessity for anxiety upon my own account.

"'I had some vague notions regarding the redemption of mankind by the atonement of Jesus Christ, but I did not clearly understand the terms of that salvation, and for a long time my heart was neither warmed by love nor touched by any sensation of fear. I did not think myself a religious or righteous man. I could not possibly deceive myself into a belief of that description. But I thought I was quite as good as many of my neighbours, and I had never been associated with the openly wicked – for whom only I regarded the wrath of God as specially reserved.

"'In this frame of mind I was turning over the leaves of the New Testament on the evening of the second Sunday of June last when my attention was suddenly and in a very unusual manner arrested by an accidental glance at the text of Hebrews 12:14. I there found stated that without holiness 'no man shall see the Lord'. That passage puzzled me. Until then I had never perceived the full meaning of it, although I must have read it fifty times before. I knew that I was without holiness and, for the first time in my life, I pondered seriously on its necessity. I asked myself what is the nature and character of the required 'holiness', and by what means may I acquire that qualification to 'see the Lord'?

"'I spent the remaining hours of that evening in deep but silent thought upon the subject, and on the course of such reflections my mind became very strangely impressed with another text, the words of which rose freshly upon my memory:– 'I am the way, the truth, and the life: no man cometh unto the Father but by Me.' I tried to find the passage but searched in vain for it. It was near midnight before I retired to bed. I was in perfect health and my mind, although seriously impressed, was not in the slightest degree agitated, but I could not sleep. I was not, nor have I ever been, superstitionally disposed but, about three o'clock when I was thoroughly awake and could see every object in the room distinctly, I felt bodily and mental sensations such as I had never previously experienced which I am unable properly to describe.

"'I felt as people are said to feel when they believe themselves to be in the presence of an invisible being. My flesh 'cracked' – a tingling thrill a sensation to me utterly unaccountable, passed through every nerve of my body. Great fear fell upon me and I could feel every hair of my head in motion. My condition must have had some points of similarity to that of Job (4:15, 16) when a Spirit 'passed before my face; the hair of my flesh stood up: It stood still, but I could not discern the form thereof: ...' At that moment soundless words were spoken within my brain. I felt then enunciated with a distinctness greater than anything that had ever fallen upon my outward ear from mortal lips.

"'The words were these – 'The wicked shall be turned into Hell, and all the nations that forget God.' I had read that passage of scripture frequently before. I had heard sermons preached from it more than once – but I never thought of it before. I knew I had forgotten God, and my eyes were instantaneously opened to a clear sight of my condition. The words impressed me, and that awakening influence upon my heart and conscience was powerful beyond description. The sensations, which I have attempted to describe, passed off within less than a single minute but their effect – their influence – I humbly trust, will abide with me to the last hour of my life. I did that morning that which I had not done for the ten years preceding it – I prayed. No human being heard me, for my lips moved not, but the language of my heart was that of a convicted sinner – I prayed that God, for Christ's sake, would 'renew a right spirit within me.'

"'I resumed my ordinary work the following day. I did not speak of my change of sentiment to any person but, for more than a month, I could not find peace of mind – no resting place for the soul of my foot. I felt humbled to the very dust and I felt so still, but I bless God that I have found help in One Who is mighty and Who is able to keep from falling all who trust in Him. I have read and heard many opinions concerning the religious revival, and I have stated my personal experience of it without reserve. I believe that it is a marvellous work of God for the conversion of souls, and may the influence of His Holy Spirit rest within every heart and soul thus quickened into life.'"

"The Coleraine Chronicle" Saturday, 15th October 1859

"We are still justified in chronicling the onward march of the religious reformation which was made manifest to all at the beginning of June, of the present year. No one can deny that a change for the better, which all must believe to be permanent, has taken place in the case of hosts of individuals who were, humanly speaking, beyond recall on the road to ruin. How many can gladly bring up to their mind's eye a reclaimed father or son, arrested on the broad path, who would have been still a domestic tyrant or a cause of reproach to a whole household, had the Almighty power of God not been put forth? How many, to take no higher standard, have clothed themselves with the money that previously supplied them with the means of pandering to their lowest and most beast-like lusts and appetites, and how few there are now – save those who would still live by the wages of iniquity – who regret the times of refreshing from the presence of the Lord, in His Own way, which hath visited us? That the Word of God has been read and studied here as it never was before will be abundantly evident when it is stated that since 1st June last, the sum received by the Coleraine Auxiliary for the Edinburgh Bible Society, for copies of the Holy Scriptures, was upwards of one hundred and eighteen pounds – about ten times as much as was ever received in the same period at any other time."

"The Ballymena Observer" Saturday, 15th October 1859

Another Fact for the Whig

"At the Crumlin Licencing sessions held this week no fewer than ten publicans declined to seek renewals, for the expressed reason that their trade had been reduced so much on account of the revival movement that they could no longer follow it profitably. Six others applied for, and obtained renewals solely in order to obtain time to dispose of their remaining stock with a view to giving up what they have reason to regard as, in that district at least, the ruining trade of a publican."

"The Armagh Gazette" Saturday, 22nd October 1859

Middletown - Priestly Intolerance

"A correspondent writing from Middletown raised the following incident of Roman intolerance in connection with the revival movement – some time ago two young girls named Susan Meaklin and Mary McClutchy, Roman Catholics, were apprenticed to two respectable persons in the village of Middletown – named Meaklin – to learn the business of dress-making. They conducted themselves with perfect propriety, and since the revival movement has sprung up they have attended several of the prayer meetings and one of them expressed a wish to join the Protestant Church. These facts came to the ears of the Roman Catholic clergy, and one of that body came to the houses of Meaklin and McClutchy and immediately ordered them to leave their employment, under certain threats and penalties, and not to dare go near anything in the shape of revivalism. This bell, book and candle system was also pursued towards all who should give work to the revivalists."

"The Ballymena Observer" Saturday, 22nd October 1859

Cootehill

"I had occasion to visit this part of the country, and was very happy to find that the work here is in a very prosperous state. Indeed, I find that in this town there has been a very great change since I visited it about three years ago. Swearing, blaspheming and drinking are scarcely known and, with regard to the last, I have been informed and I believe on good authority that five spirit sellers will give up their licences in consequence.

"Another good feature here is the unanimity among the people – there is a prayer meeting every night. One night it is held in the Established Church, another in the Wesleyan Methodist Chapel and another in one of the Presbyterian churches, where all mix together, both clergy and laity of the several denominations. I was very much pleased last night at one of the meetings in the Methodist Chapel. When I entered I was greatly surprised to see the Rev. Mr. Bones, the Presbyterian minister, occupying a chair, and the house as might have been expected was quite full. All seemed desirous of obtaining the blessing."

"The Ballymena Observer" Saturday, 5ᵗʰ November 1859

The Sign of the Times

"We observe, it is stated, that Messrs. McKenzie's Distillery, Belfast, one of the most complete in Ireland and capable of turning out one million two hundred thousand gallons per year, is for sale by auction. And if not sold as a distillery is to be dismantled, and sold piecemeal. The distillery at Hillsborough is also for sale. If manufacturers of whiskey in the North of Ireland were a 'profiting' trade, as once it was particularly in the Great Belfast Distillery before revival days, neither of the businesses mentioned would be long in the market."

The Maze Races – The Revival

"On Wednesday last, these races (October meeting) were held as usual at the Maze. Although the day was fine, and there was a well filled card, the course was all but abandoned – five hundred we are told were all that could be mustered on the occasion, where formerly it was no unusual thing to see perhaps ten to fifteen thousand people with the usual supply of tumblers, conjurers and thimble riggers. In the midst of a district where the revival flourished, and is still continuing, we can ascribe the desertion of the racecourse to no other cause than the impression religion has made upon men's minds.

"'Not a single case of drunkenness was to be seen' says the Whig – 'Yesterday (Wednesday) the business of the October meeting commenced at the Maze. There was a very well filled card for the principal event of the day – the Queen's Plate of one hundred guineas, and the weather, with a little warmth in the atmosphere would have been quite the sort for a racecourse, for the day was dry and remarkably clear, but intensely cold throughout. At least one good race might have been expected. In fact, the Maze had very little of its normal appearance. The tents were reduced to one, which sat upon the hill in isolation. The crowd outside did not exceed five thousand. Good order, however, prevailed and there was not a case of drunkenness to be seen. So much for the effects of the revival.'"

"The Ballymena Observer" Saturday, 24ᵗʰ December 1859

"We have recently had various communications from England and Scotland and continuing enquiries concerning the present state of the religious movement in this neighbourhood. We have requested a statement of facts concerning the revival from the Rev. Fredrick Buick, the respected Pastor of the 2ⁿᵈ Presbyterian Church, Ahoghill. He has kindly favoured us with a reply and we publish it as a general answer to our correspondence:–

"'Dear Sir, as you have asked me for information respecting the present state of revival at Ahoghill and its neighbourhood, I proceed to comply with your request.

"'After making minute enquiry of those who have been connected with the revival from its commencement as to its present state in their districts, it is their universal and decided testimony that the truths are still abiding without any symptoms of decline. There are some few cases of inconsistency and of returning back again to their former state and habits, but these are extremely few – indeed the wonder is that they are so few.

"'Meeting a gentleman today from the ferry who takes a deep interest in the work, who has fitted up one of his lofts for religious services weekly and who knows the country well – on being asked if the work was keeping steady, he replied that the interest in the revival instead of declining was on the increase and, on further enquiry, he said he was satisfied the work was of God and its fruit permanent.

"'Regarding another district, the testimony of an intelligent, godly, earnest man, who has been revived himself and his whole family, is that the awakened and converted are progressing in knowledge and in grace. Before the introduction of the revival he was sorely distressed with his sons who were wild, reckless and godless. He could not get them, by any persuasion, to attend to the things of God. These young men are now nightly in the scriptures, powerful in prayer and their whole delight is centred in Jesus. Now they are one of the happiest families. They have one heart and one way. Their joy is unbounded and their praise is continually of Divine grace.

"'An aged believer whose religious affections have been greatly revived says of his locality that their work is still progressing. At the prayer meeting, of which he is a leader, there is no abatement of interest. Lately there has been an unusual excitement. The Spirit has been breathing upon the dry bones. During the time of the revival there were times when this good man felt such a power of love that he was forced to cry out, 'Lord, restrain Thy Hand, I can bear no more.'

"'It is truly astonishing to witness the deep solemnity which pervades the whole deportment of many who, before conversion, were regardless of Divine things. Now their appearance is that of an all-pervading seriousness. Now how they have been subdued, changed and solemnised! Their growth in knowledge is rapid, their love of the Bible intense and it is marvellous to hear with what unction and power they can approach the Throne of Grace in prayer. They are called to be saints.

"'Some twelve months ago no person could have imagined, nor could the announcement have been credited, that so many prayer meetings would have started up in the most unfavourable localities, conducted as they have been with solemnity and to the great edification of people from whom nothing of the kind could have been expected – yet so it is. Behold, what has God wrought?

"'It is the general impression that a work of grace has been going on silently and without observation in the hearts of hundreds through the country, who have had no bodily prostrations. It is known by the feeling of deep solemnity that pervades the neighbourhood – by the vast increase of family religion – by the absence of previous prevailing sins – by the keeping up of prayer meetings in almost every locality – by the great increase in the attendance on the ordinances of God's House. The three Presbyterian churches in Ahoghill are full, and the 2nd and 3rd are contemplating large additions to their accommodation.

"'The Lord has done great things for us. We thank God and take courage to work and wait, still crying with the agonising cry of faith, 'Wilt Thou not revive us again, that Thy people may rejoice and be glad in Thee?' - Faithfully yours, F. Buick.'"

Revival Movement Association and Every Home Crusade

Revival Publishing is a branch of Revival Movement Association which is an Interdenominational Evangelistic Mission. This ministry was commenced sixty years ago. Our work involves publishing and printing gospel literature in over ninety languages. This literature is supplied free of charge to many Missions, Churches, Pastors and Christian workers in over one hundred and twenty countries.

We have our own printing equipment and on average use four tonnes of paper each day on our presses. Each year we print over nine million Gospels of John and many millions of Scripture booklets as we believe in the importance of the Word of God. We also produce gospel tracts and sets of Children's Bible Lessons.

Today many Christians desire to evangelise with gospel literature but it is either not available or is too expensive. We would like to share with you the thrill of what the Lord is doing in our world through this literature and the challenge we face in supplying our brothers and sisters with sufficient quantities. If you would like more information please write to us or visit our website www.revivalmovement.org.